The Concept of
Corporate Strategy

The Concept of Corporate Strategy

KENNETH R. ANDREWS
Donald Kirk David Professor of
Business Administration
Harvard University

1971
DOW JONES-IRWIN, INC.
Homewood, Illinois 60430

Library of Congress Catalog Card No. 75–153173

Printed in the United States of America

To
Edmund P. and Zella R. Learned

Preface

THIS SMALL BOOK is devoted to the large subject of Business Policy. It is addressed primarily to the important class of businessmen and women who run our companies or corporations. This group, unevenly qualified by education and experience but uniformly burdened by the same kind of responsibility, is made elite not by inheritance or schooling but by its assigned duties. Its members have responsibility for leading the organizations that develop material wealth in our society and thereby make possible all the other kinds of wealth that constitute our civilization and make life worthwhile. Those who hold or aspire to general management positions and membership in this group should find here some ideas to help them realize, acquire, or at least articulate the goal-setting and policy-making processes in which their busy lives are caught up. These ideas bear directly on the central problems of corporate chairmen and presidents, members of boards of directors, executive and functional vice presidents, and general managers of autonomous divisions or profit centers. The concepts presented here will also be of interest to some others —including those specialists who realize that no particular expertness can ever be brought to full flower except by experts who also have some kind of generalist capacity.

The substance of some of this book has appeared before (sometimes in the same words) in *Business Policy: Text and Cases,* published first by Richard D. Irwin, Inc., in 1965 and reissued in a revised edition in 1969. That volume, the joint work of Edmund P. Learned, C. Roland Christensen, William D. Guth, and myself, is widely used in Business Policy courses in business schools both in graduate and executive programs. Interest in the text has extended outside schools and company seminars. The original text is now issued in this somewhat extended form to make it available to the general reader without the burden of the accompanying cases. It becomes available now also to students who are using cases other than the selection we have offered in our earlier books.

Business Policy as a generic term designates the field of professional study sometimes called "General Management," "Top Management," "Strategic Action in the Total Enterprise," or "Enterprise Direction." It is the study of the functions and responsibilities of those charged with running a successful business or a multifunctional entity within it. The problems studied affect the character and success of the entire company. They have to do with the choice of objectives, the molding of organizational capability and character, the definition of what needs to be done, and the mobilization of resources for the attainment of goals. Their urgency as problems increases sharply amid changing circumstances, shifts of demand, competitive countermoves, and scarcities of skill or capital. Like "national policy," "public policy," or "foreign policy," *busi-*

ness policy is an intermixture of goals and purposes, impediments and obstacles, threats and opportunities, resources
and applications, environmental information and misinfor-
mation which serves as the context of strategic decision in
a tumult of competition. The successful resolution of dis-
order in the jumble of environmental forces, goals, and
resources is what policy formulation is all about.

Although it may be difficult to make the term immediately clear to those who are not accustomed to using it,
Business Policy as a field of professional education for management has occupied for 60 years an important place in
the curriculum of the Harvard Business School. There a
considerable group of teachers and researchers sustain an
integrative capstone course in general management devoted to the problems of the firm as a whole as seen from
the perspective of the general manager or chief executive.
Its traditional format includes complex cases, continually
renewed, presenting as far as practicable the total situation of a firm at or over a period of time. The student is
asked to analyze the situation, to isolate and identify the
principal problems in it, and to prescribe a program of
action including attention to both the problems and opportunities available to the firm.

A man[1] is required to do all this in the hope that he will
be usefully equipped thereby for practical experience in
two different ways. First, he receives training in what the
problems of general management are in such a way that
he cannot remain blind to the varying contribution his own
specialty may be expected to make as priorities shift among
the problems of his firm. Second, we hope he becomes bet-

---

[1] In these days of feminine sensitivity to male chauvinism and discrimination against women in management, let it be clear that when
I say a man in the abstract, I usually mean in shorthand a *man or
woman,* just as the term *mankind* includes women.

ter able to learn from experience how to be a general manager, should his abilities and experience lead him in this direction. The second outcome requires more than just exposure to cases and the drill of situational analysis. A conceptual scheme for comprehending the variety of separate cases and situations is also required—one general enough to span the enormous variety of business activity and problems, yet potent enough to permit a knowledgeable, systematic, and effective approach to any one situation. The unifying concept which makes sense out of the confusion of responsibility in which any general manager finds himself is the principal subject of this book.

Before we address directly the formulation and execution of corporate strategy—for this is the concept to which I refer—a word or two more may throw some light on the credentials which this idea carries. It has evolved as the unifying theory underlying years of the firsthand field study of by now many hundreds of business organizations. These are mostly American firms, but since 1957 our researchers have done field work, project research, consultation, and case studies in Central America, England, France, Germany, Holland, India, Italy, Sweden, and Switzerland. Our colleagues at other American universities and at institutions in Mexico, Spain, and Brazil have lengthened this list to many more Western countries. A doctoral research program has produced a succession of more theoretical studies which are extending and developing our model of the general management function. Postdoctoral project research has produced a number of important books, the most recent of which are *Industrial Planning in France,* by John H. McArthur and Bruce R. Scott; and *Managing the Resource Allocation Process: A Study of Corporate Planning and Investment,* by Joseph L. Bower.

In addition to their teaching and research, all members

of this investigative cadre serve as consultants or directors in business organizations in planned exposure to responsibility intended to enhance their familiarity with strategic decision. The understanding of management which this kind of observation has provided them is certainly incomplete, but it is clearly linked to reality. Our theory of management is neither elegant nor esoteric but it relates (1) to business life as it is, as well as (2) to what it may become. The second of these is more important to us than the first, but the first remains indispensable to the second. Ignorance or contempt of present reality is a poor basis for future improvement.

What are former students of this field supposed to have gained from it? Although it is difficult to separate the impact of a single course of study, especially when it is supposed to integrate more specialized subdivisions of management, we should look at what Business Policy is supposed to do for those who study it. I have already said that it provides direct but distant preparation for performance as general manager and requires the immediate broadening of the provincial perspective of the specialist. In addition it should result in certain knowledge, attitudes, and skills relevant to these benefits.

The *knowledge* is principally the uses of the concept of strategy and the concept itself. We will have much to say about this shortly.

The *attitudes,* which may be second nature to anyone who has read this far, include, first, acceptance of the frustrations and satisfactions of the orientation we call *generalist.* Secondly, we prescribe the point of view of the practitioner rather than that of the scholar or scientist—the thinking, intelligent, and learning practitioner, it should be said at once—not the complacent and obsolescent intuitionist. We deal in the willingness to act in the fact of incomplete information and to run the risk of being proved wrong by subsequent events. With no special fondness for overconfidence or the impulse to act without analysis, we like even less organizational drifting or individual hesitation in the face of the managerial imperative to make direction-determining decisions. Thirdly, we assume the orientation of the professional manager as distinct from the self-serving contriver of deals. We admire quick response to opportunity and entrepreneurial energy, but we intend to apply mind and judgment to such elemental gifts. We acknowledge as well the considerable obligation of the business community to the rest of society. Finally, the indoctrination and attitudes we think appropriate to business leadership include a preference for creativity and innovation over the maintenance of the status quo. Everyone naturally likes proprietary monopoly and patentable invention when it can be secured. We like to think that imagination can be applied less dramatically but with impressive results to every aspect of conducting a dynamic business, especially its adaptation to changing circumstance.

Policy skills which readers of this book may or may not see in those who have formally studied Business Policy are both analytic and administrative. Schools are better able to develop analytical power than administrative ability. It is experience in the latter that communicates finally to all the enormous importance of administration and to some a modest competence in it. The diagnostician of the total situation of a firm must understand the relation of problems to each other without dependence on a single discipline like finance, accounting, engineering, marketing, production, or organizational behavior. He must be able to deal with problems less structured than those of the special fields. He must be able to see and devise patterns of information, activities, and relationships, for if a man in a gen-

eral management position deals one at a time with the facts
he is given or the problems and staff-recommended solutions he receives, he risks being overwhelmed. But above
all, he must superimpose design upon the activities of his
company and relate it successfully to its environment. This
effort entails, as we shall see, the ability to identify significant trends in that environment and to estimate future
opportunity and risk for firms of varying resources and
competence. He must know how to appraise the capability
of his own company, to determine the strength it must develop, to predict the impact of his own action on that of
his competitors. The highest function of the general manager is supervision of the continuous process of determining the nature of the enterprise and setting, revising, and
attempting to achieve its goals. The skills involved in the
successful strategic decision occur rarely. They are of great
value in a burgeoning world which would be lost without
the power of organized effort. This interesting fact makes
these skills worthy of pursuit. It does not at all justify the
self-defeating assumption that they cannot really be studied, identified, and systematically developed.

Readers of this book are well aware of how much opportunity exists to improve the management of their own
and most other organizations and of how little conscious
and effective attention is given to the identification of alternative purposes and to a reasoned choice among them.
They should find the reference to the kind of knowledge,
attitudes, and skills which comprise the orderly study of
Policy appropriate to their own responsibilities and opportunities. But it is of course true that the study of Business Policy as defined here has application beyond the institutions of what we sometimes call free enterprise.
Officers of the civilian and military agencies of our own
and foreign governments and the managers of hospitals,

foundations, universities, and other nonprofit organizations have responded repeatedly at executive programs to the analogies between their own situations and those of their peers in business. Deciding what an organization should do and getting it done are the universal functions of an organization leader, in business or out.

It is interesting to note that the approaches to the strategic opportunity of organizations are applicable as well to individual lives and careers. Choice of goals and the achievement of sufficient personal commitment to those goals to sustain a lifetime of productive contribution to all the groups to which we belong can be a vital personal as well as professional activity. It is clearly appropriate for the person struggling with a definition of organization purpose to inquire into the relationship of that effort to his own personal goals. Whenever he is brought face to face (as who is not at one time or another) with the question, "What am I doing this for?" he has arrived at a crisis of assessment which requires the kind of knowledge, judgment, and decision of which policy making is comprised.

The construction of a practitioner's theory of general management is a difficult task made attractive by its manifest usefulness, in business or outside it, to the very valuable people who accept and attempt to discharge executive responsibility. The biases and values affecting this book have begun to appear and will continue to be clear throughout. The preference for conscious purpose over opportunism, without neglecting fortuitous development, is implicit in all that is said here. The conviction that the management of organized activity is one of the world's most important functions and one of man's highest skills also inheres in everything that follows. That business management is not only a vital profession but one that grows constantly in both complexity and manifest competence is also my conviction. People who do not believe that management is an activity requiring at its best extraordinary intellect and intelligence, marked physical powers in terms of energy, stamina, and strength, and durable moral qualities like courage, integrity, determination, and ability to choose right over wrong should read no further, for nothing in the pages to come will make sense to them. All others are welcome. For them there should be some of the same stimulation that usually attends teaching and research in Business Policy.

Needless to say, this book is far more a record of the work of others than an original document of my own, just as before it the notes in *Business Policy: Text and Cases* were. I have participated in all the work reflected here for many years, but the concept of corporate strategy presented in these pages is first an evocation and articulation of what has been implied in generations of empirical studies in our university. Second, it is the joint property of a lively group of seasoned and young practitioners and scholars of this decade. My own membership in this group will not prevent me from praising it for the brains and verve with which it doggedly pursues the most difficult problems of business administration. Names from the near and more distant past include the late George Albert Smith, Jr., and Melvin T. Copeland, Georges Doriot, Richard Merriam, Edmund P. Learned, all now retired. They have been followed by a company whose variety, independence, and individuality have not obscured a slowly progressive evolution of conceptual insight into phenomena very patiently studied in the setting of unique situations. C. Roland Christensen, an extraordinarily gifted teacher, researcher, and corporate director-consultant, is currently chairman of this group. Robert W. Austin, Charles A.

Bliss, Wilbur B. England, Myles L. Mace, John D. Glover, Robert W. Merry, and Clarence B. Nickerson have all at one time or another been full-time professors of Policy and have maintained their interest in the subject. Several of our recent colleagues, like William D. Guth and David C. D. Rogers are now teaching Policy in other universities. Currently Robert W. Ackerman, Francis J. Aguilar, Norman A. Berg, Joseph L. Bower, John B. Matthews, Malcolm F. Salter, Bruce R. Scott, John W. Rosenblum, Audrey T. Sproat, Hugo E. R. Uyterhoeven, and Michael von Clemm comprise the central group. In a professional school sympathetic to the practice of management, most faculty members retain an interest in Policy which parallels their expertness in a class of more specific management problems. Although it is impracticable to name this large number, from their interest we have profited a good deal in ways which add to all the Policy group's pride in belonging to the Faculty of the Harvard Business School. To these persons and the many company presidents and officers who have helped them by admitting them to observation or participation in the processes by which strategic decisions are made or defaulted, belongs the idea which in this book I will try to make clear. My shortcomings in so doing will be noticed and no doubt challenged by my colleagues; they may be thus spurred to their own attempt to communicate to others outside our classroom, consulting, and research circles what so thoroughly fascinates and provocatively informs all of us.

To former Dean George P. Baker and his successor, Dean Lawrence E. Fouraker, I am grateful not only for their support of Policy studies generally but for making it possible for me to complete this book.

April, 1971   KENNETH R. ANDREWS

Contents

The Importance of
Being General

BEFORE EMBARKING upon an extended definition of the
concept of corporate strategy, we should first examine the
peculiar functions of the general manager. We must note
that for the highest responsibility in the hierarchy of management little formal training is available. Indeed, some
of the general manager's previous executive and technical
experience may be, if anything, incapacitating. More ur-
gently, we must consider the general manager's need to
rely for his principal support on a tier of functional managers, each more knowledgeable than himself within a
particular area, each fortified by a pride in his own expertness bred of our highly technical society, each thus correspondingly doubtful of the primacy of the generalist role,
and each committed—perhaps overcommitted to further-
ing the interests of his own function. Under these circum-

1

stances, the functional specialist must be regarded not only as a resource but also as a problem in communication, direction, and control.

Given both the challenge and the difficulties of his position, the general manager is in need of whatever help we can provide. One form that assistance might take is to offer a conceptual framework for thinking about the problems that confront the general manager, breaking his problems down into more manageable units, and proposing a sequence in which they might be reasonably ranked and considered. Essentially, it is the function of this whole book to provide such a framework as this, and the function of this chapter to set this framework in the larger perspective of the needs it might meet and the uses it might serve.

FUNCTIONS OF THE GENERAL MANAGER

Management itself may be regarded as leadership in the informed, planned, purposeful conduct of complex organized activity. General management is the management of a total enterprise or an autonomous subunit. The term *general manager* thus embraces the chief executive officer of the organization; members of the office of the president; executive and senior vice presidents who have interfunctional responsibilities; and presidents or managers of divisions, multifunctional profit centers, and similar partially autonomous organization units. The point of view of general management, though not its full practice, is also essential to others—to outside directors, financial analysts, consultants, for example, who cannot accurately evaluate general management without knowing what it is. A total organization perspective is also important to senior functional officers whose concern is more for the contribution their subspecialists make to the operating organization than for the technical complexity of their work.

The practitioner of general management—who has, as we shall see, four sets of responsibilities—is looked to first and most often to achieve results in the present, to produce against continually rising expectations of planned earnings per share and return on the shareholders' investment. In supervising current operations to this end, the general manager is expected to remain continually informed and ready to intervene in crises. Beyond coping with emergencies, he is expected on a day-to-day basis to take part in divisional or corporate ceremonial activities, to receive visitors of his own stature from abroad and from other companies, and to entertain important customers. Between trips he will see in his own office far more people who want to see him than he would ever take the initiative to see. If he has operations in other countries or states, he is expected to visit these periodically. Because circumstance and competition constantly churn up emergencies, today almost always takes precedence in his working life over tomorrow, and the short run usually crowds out the long haul. Presiding over current operations always takes more time than anyone thinks it should. His reputation and rewards ride on current results which others may have largely determined, purposefully or unwittingly, years before.

In addition to maintaining surveillance over the actual attainment of results formally or informally planned, the general manager is usually expected to make himself or at least to preside over the process of making policy decisions affecting future results. This activity entails choosing or tacitly ratifying a choice of goals and performing some kind of planning function which insures that these goals have some chance of being achieved on schedule. He consents to and often intervenes in investment decisions which have a cumulative impact, planned or not, on the nature of his total enterprise. He is generally less captain of the future than of the present, but more than anyone else in his organization he is responsible for setting direction, and for undertaking today activities which succeed or fail in delivering results tomorrow. Although consideration of all the alternatives available for the growth and progress of a dynamic and diversified manufacturing firm might well take more time by itself than that available to him and to his planning staff, he is usually able to devote far less time to planning than almost everybody else thinks he should.

But achieving results from current operations and planning to achieve future results of greater or different dimensions are only part of the general manager's extensive jurisdiction. The chief executive of a unit or a total organization is expected to develop and change its structure and to deploy its people in such a way as to permit both business success and individual satisfaction and expression, and to secure both *effectiveness* and *efficiency*, in Chester Barnard's terms. The general manager presides over systems of intended cooperation which produce inevitable conflict to be resolved. He is continually pressed by his subordinates to make decisions he may not be ready to make. If, as is normal in a healthy organization, his plans include growth or his success in operations forces expansion, he must make painful decisions to remove or reassign persons whose development has not kept pace, so as to open the way for younger and better qualified managers. As sophistication in management rises and the qualifications and expectations of young people also rise, he must make his company attractive to recruits, keep opportunity for young people open, and make his organization a stimulating and interesting place in which to work. He is constantly confronted with a need to do things easier left undone. He is called upon to evaluate as well as to encourage, and to penalize as well as to reward. In consequence he is faced with extraordinary difficulties in gaining timely knowledge of what really is going on, for people in organizations protect themselves against evaluation. With such knowledge as comes to him through formal and personal means, he supervises the optimum integration of the specialized functions or departments of his organization and supplies them with the resources appropriate to the contribution they are expected to make. He is not generally much recognized for his contribution to organization, and the pressure for results he must exert upon it may not make him much loved.

The general manager is thus responsible for the success of the business, for the quality and effectiveness of its present and future success in competition, and for solutions to the economic and human problems attending even the most humdrum production of goods and services. He is usually expected to make a personal as well as an official contribution to group effort, to excel in some technical or social way, and to demonstrate continually to his board and to his "inside public" that he deserves to be in the position he occupies. His manner of leading, of which much more will be said in Chapter 8, is expected to color in some way the character and image of his organization. When he is ready to retire or move on, he is supposed to have someone ready to take his place who is even more preeminent in some important way.

So far, we have touched lightly on the general manager's four-sided responsibility to supervise current operations, plan future operations, coordinate the functions and human capabilities of his organization, and make a distinctive personal contribution. All this obviously constitutes a heavy burden. Quite apart from the technical complexity of the tactical decisions he must make in response to competitive moves and the subtlety required to develop an organization more and more capable of both reaching targets and providing satisfying careers for people, the general manager is expected by his family to play as full a role as father and husband as his human qualities suggest is possible and necessary. His industry expects him to be active in its trade association. His local community expects him to appear at least in such conventional roles of good citizenship as the chairman of hospital and charity boards and drives. If he becomes well known, his national government grows more and more interested in enlisting him in task forces to address the nation's social and economic problems. His university expects him to be of executive as well as material assistance to its activities. Meanwhile, everybody expects him to take the measures necessary to maintain his health and vigor. As a consequence, we are forced to face the familiar irony that as a man progresses in power and prestige and approaches the highest position in his own hierarchy of opportunity and reward, he is less and less a master of his own life and must work harder than most of his juniors. The sheer unorganized profusion of what is required of the general manager sends some gifted men into obsessive preoccupation with their work or into frenetic schedules which frustrate their families, subordinates, and associates. Such men have no time to read books on how to organize their days and little opportunity to feel the full satisfaction which a balanced discharge of their duties should render. The man not especially equipped for this welter of activity is likely to end up either warped, in some areas inactive and ineffective, tired, or prematurely dead.

The Origins and Development of General Managers

The full catalog of general management activity, hardly sketched here, suggests why a scarcity of the requisite general management ability is felt in all earnest and honest organizations. The sense of shortage is due not only to the constructive discontent that leads superior organizations and people to aspire to higher and higher levels of accomplishment. It is also due to the hardly disputable fact that a clear majority of businesses, in even the most sophisticated economy in the world, are mismanaged in some obvious and preventable ways. We allocate an improperly complex set of tasks to our general managers, or we follow an inadequate system for preparing likely candidates—one or the other or both.

It is evident at once that little special effort is directed to the education of general managers, and that little opportunity is afforded either in education or in industry to specialize in generality. In the graduate schools of business, courses in general management have usually occupied a very small segment of the curriculum; in some graduate schools, preeminent in older disciplines like economics, management is taught hardly at all and may even be asserted to be unteachable. In any case, only a small proportion of present-day chief executives and probably only a slightly larger proportion of divisional and profit-center managers have undergone prior professional training for their responsibilities. At most, even these few have had very little exposure. The university executive programs which have flourished since World War II have brought effective broadening to a larger number of managers in senior positions, but the brevity of these programs necessarily limits their contribution, effective as inquiry shows it to have been.[1] The infinite variety of business activity across industries, countries, and firms large and small, makes it difficult to educate men in general management except through practice.

Beyond the business schools, themselves unequal to the problem, our educational system, which should and perhaps does at times produce potential generalists from colleges of liberal arts, often seems to turn men away from business or from vigorous action and leadership of any sort. The link between liberal education and the life of action, which might provide the best initial preparation for general management responsibility, is much less obvious than the tie between the departments in which students major and the graduate departments to which the best students tend to go.

Schools of law, engineering, and foreign service have been unintentionally successful in preparing some of their graduates for ultimate careers as general managers in business. Their curricula, however, do not contain concepts, approaches, or even much knowledge specifically directed at coping with the general manager's problem. Some more direct preparation, not necessitating a change in profession, would be desirable. Lest this point be misunderstood, it should be repeated: that such professional business schools as teach *management* rather than disciplines in some way *related* to management, and that offer executive programs, do provide direct preparation. But the dis-

---

[1]See Kenneth R. Andrews, *The Effectiveness of University Management Development Programs* (Boston: Harvard Business School Division of Research, 1965).

crepancy between the extent and impact of this effort and the total number of and need for general managers is still very great.

The problem of previous preparation and systematic development of general management potential goes beyond the schools; it extends into business itself. Even the most biased educator would admit that professional experience, from which professional education can prepare one to learn effectively and quickly, is far more potent than the classroom in preparing men for professional responsibility. Despite the appearance of highly decentralized or divisionalized profit-center organizations, it is unreasonable to expect that a young man can step directly into general management responsibility without having passed through—and having been marked by—effective and usually outstanding performance as a functional specialist. The first assignment as a general manager, to oversimplify somewhat, is like the first ski jump. It cannot really be approached so gradually as to avoid one big step at last.

Decentralized organizations, notably General Electric for one, do provide hundreds of general manager positions in product departments which require multifunctional responsibility on a limited and extensively staff-supported scale. Such companies, as at least General Electric does, provide opportunity to participate in both university and company general management courses of up to two or three months in length. In addition, the young candidate for such positions, if identified early enough, can be rotated among the sections of his product department—marketing, manufacturing, engineering, control, finance, industrial relations—enough to insure that he does not embark upon his multifunctional responsibility with a single-function bias. But functional assignments are so complex technically that a man cannot easily prove himself in a specialty for which he has not been prepared, nor can he demonstrate in a short time by superior performance in two or three specialties that he is of general management caliber. It is interesting to note that we are much more demanding of precise and specific training and experience in the major functional specialties than in general management.

But sink or swim is one of the oldest of educational techniques. Why should we not be satisfied with the process of placing promising young men into positions of responsibility and letting them succeed or fail? The essential problem in this approach is the problem of measurement—how to tell whether the new general manager is doing well or badly. The new general manager, on probation in a profit center, is usually evaluated like his seniors, primarily by the results he is credited with, i.e., the bottom line of the quarterly operating statement during the time he is in office. In a technical and competitive manufacturing business, his present profit is actually a composite not only of the capability of his organization, which he may not be able to alter immediately, but of decisions to reinvest new capital and what otherwise would be profits in strategic expenses years before. If his predecessor's general management capability was also measured largely by his own current performance, he may have done what his successor is now tempted to do— borrow from a hazy future development and sacrifice future stability and profit to produce vividly attractive current returns. If the young executive succumbs to the temptation to look good in the short run and this fact is not subsequently detected by his superiors—who, after all, have told him that he is free to do whatever he elects so long as he achieves planned results—then our young man may succeed so well that he is promoted to a higher general management position, leaving his successor to be penalized some years hence. The general manager is safely measured by current results only when he remains in office for a considerable period of time. We should note in passing the need for more useful criteria than current results in evaluating general management performance. This need will bring us back to the subject in Chapter 7. In the meantime we should note that exposing a large number of high-potential men to actual responsibility and letting results designate the survivors is deceptively attractive. Such a practice must be accompanied by sensitive supervision of the ex-specialist, who must learn somehow, from what he does and from what his bosses and subordinates tell him, what constitutes a successful, balanced performance of the total general management job.

The general manager in any position—at the head of a small profit center or a large corporation—who would take his own development in hand is not, to be sure, without resources. If he has studied general management functions in graduate school or in one of the now numerous company-sponsored general management programs, and if his job experience has acquainted him with at least the importance of other specialties than his own, he has taken some important steps. Assuming he retains his zest for general management and for what he perceives are its rewards in power, status, excitement, and money, he probably knows, for example, that just because marketing may be the single most important function, given his business and the nature of competition, that he cannot run his profit center as an ex-marketer. He knows also that the engineering, manufacturing, and product development people of his organization do not necessarily acknowledge the dominance of marketing, and that they make budget demands appropriate to their own concept of their function and its importance. His awareness and motivation thus prepare him to read, observe, listen, and learn.

The young generalist, in quest of guidance on the kind of decisions he should be making to fulfill his functions as achiever of results, direction setter, organization head, and personal leader, will find many sources of ostensible instruction. The advice he will be offered most persistently by his seniors will be the conventional wisdom of the industry—the way a railroad, insurance company, construction firm, farm equipment manufacturer, or steel producer is run and always has been run. All his knowledgeable informants will, for example, revise the action implications of their new market studies in the light of either industry judgments or the decisions of industry leaders. After all, who knows more about automobiles than General Motors, about aluminum than ALCOA, about glass containers than Owens-Illinois? Our general manager will naturally examine and perhaps imitate not only the general management decisions of his competitors and elders, but perhaps their personal style as well. If his industry is well managed and well led, he should be well instructed and should be able to maintain his inherited market share and about the same average return on investment as the rest of his industry. He is not likely to be innovative, aggressive, or successful in solving chronic industry problems through this approach, but it will vastly simplify his life and lighten his schedule. When the fortunes of his firm dwindle in interindustry competition, he will be in good company.

If our prototype general manager has higher goals and reads or listens to his educated subordinates and consultants, he may well encounter management scientists who will claim or imply that operations research, simulation, mathematical modeling, statistical decision theory, and other approaches made possible by the computer can make important improvements in operating efficiency and a more orderly consideration of alternative future courses of action. Arrayed against the management scientists are a surviving band of pragmatists who believe that if you take care of today well enough, tomorrow will take care of itself, or that muddling through—preferably muddling through with a purpose felt but not clearly stated—is a more realistic way to approach policy decisions, as indicated in H. Edward Wrapp's "Good Managers Don't Make Policy Decisions."[2] There is a school of organization theorists who also believe that the general manager does not so much make as recognize, ratify, or be made captive by decisions emerging out of powerful organization processes not easily interrupted. The manager should give top priority, in this prescription, to so influencing the climate that effective decisions emerge, no matter how their effectiveness is judged at the time. In this case also the future of the company evolves, this time even less under direct guidance by the general manager than by the intuitive pragmatist, in a way that is at least natural if not predetermined by rational choice of systematically studied opportunities.

If the general manager who would develop a better way to manage were to listen to subordinates representing older functions than the newer varieties of quantitative analysis, he would hear proposals that resources should be devoted to the function in effect for the function's sake or to the division for the division's sake—all such argu-

---

[2]*Harvard Business Review,* September-October, 1967, pp. 91–99.

ments made persuasive by references to past history, the status quo, personal and organization relationships, and all colored by an inability to assess clearly whether the function was indeed performing its essential role or whether the division should be continued in business at all. His planning staff will harp on the need to develop five- and ten-year plans that may or may not seem to him to be unnecessarily detailed and rigidly confident that today's assumptions and conditions will be valid tomorrow. And somewhere in his organization will be one or more frustrated entrepreneurs with favorite proposals for new ventures in radical new businesses via expensive internal development or acquisition which have no other organizational support at all.

In addition to the advice and instruction of uncertain value available from these quarters, bold suggestions for reform, development, or new directions flow in from a considerable number of government and academic observers. These sources call attention to both the unfulfilled obligations which they allege business has accumulated and the new opportunities for profitable enterprise now open to business in such fields as education, low-cost housing, purification of atmosphere and water, and other control of social and physical environmental conditions.

In short, general management has no established system of recruitment, education, or on-the-job training appropriate to its great dimensions. If the additional recommendations presented in this book are to be of concrete help, they must of necessity provide for the development of a point of view appropriate to the needs and opportunities of the generalist and for a concept of his role which reduces the multiplicity of tasks now heaped upon him to a reasonable life's work. We have long since learned that the practice of management is not well served by specifying the extraordinary personal qualities appropriate to ideal casting. Managers, like lawyers and doctors, are people with a high minimum of important shared basic qualities amid an infinity of personality differences. Far more important than the intelligence, integrity, energy, and courage which their assignments require and which are hard enough to find are the skills of mind and action which convert these qualities in quite individualistic ways into impressive performance.

IMPORTANCE OF THE GENERALIST IN A WORLD OF SPECIALISTS

Both our failure to establish a tradition of specific preparation for general management responsibilities and our casual selection of candidates for this post on the basis of effective past performance of a specialty (which may require few of the coordinating skills needed for overall leadership) bespeak an historic disrespect for the pretensions of general management to being a specialty of its own. The almost incredible accomplishments of present-day industry are to most eyes the consequences of technology, which is in the hands of an enormous corps of well-educated specialists. Where once a fairly technical business needed only a few functional specialists in research and development, engineering, manufacturing, marketing, labor relations, finance, and accounting, now each of the major functions of business has been subdivided into many more subspecialties. Major new functions have come into being. The area of marketing, for example, has produced specialists in market research, consumer behavior, statistical methods, advertising, merchandising and promotion, sales management, procurement, and distribution. The reason is, of course, the desire to bring to bear on a total task the knowledge which must necessarily be rigidly circumscribed in breadth if it is to be mastered in depth. The narrowness of a specialty makes sense in two ways. Being circumscribed, the specialty can be mastered by an individual and extended by research and practice by a group of individuals all agreeing on parameters, assumptions, and definitions. The way in which a specialty is circumscribed makes possible, furthermore, a feasible assignment for an individual—both in learning what needs to be known, staying abreast of developments, and applying that knowledge to the small class of problems it fits.

Specialization and subspecialization make possible a meaningful division of labor which enables a small organization to accomplish feats far beyond even large numbers of unspecialized persons. The very fecundity with which special fields are created and nourished has captured the imagination of recent generations. The marvels of accomplishment which come from the specialties lead most people to prize exact knowledge and demonstrable expertness in an admittedly limited field and by contrast perhaps to downgrade the more general and less tangible skills of integrating specialized performance into a profit-making, self-perpetuating, organic whole. The expert, challenged to demonstrate skill in a game in which the rules are clear, develops a proficiency which tends to make him contemptuous of whose who do not have it. Usefully morale-inducing as motivation, this pride in specialty easily becomes arrogance and narrowness. At best, it is neither possible nor desirable to expect experts to forgo their point of view or to avoid collision with other points of view. Experts from different disciplines will seldom agree, for their frame of reference engenders different observations and conclusions.

The differences in point of view among specialized functions and between every specialized function and general management must be accepted as inevitable. To the inconvenient and frustrating inevitability of conflicts among specialists no solution is immediately available. Ultimately, if the value of the general management function becomes more widely recognized in the universities (themselves currently in disruption and danger because of poor administration arising in part from faculty denigration of the management function), students of business and the professions may be required during their course of study to develop some generalist capacity. Education may eventually grant the importance of the general purposes in the real world to which specialized knowledge must be applied. Until that unlikely day arrives it is the administrators of practical affairs who must educate the experts in the art of being useful when the tasks to be done do not fall neatly into the purview of a single function.

The experts needing this attention are many. They include, for example, the accountant whose approach to preparation of monthly statements is meticulously detailed, rigidly accurate, formalistically correct, and therefore so long delayed as to be useless to managers; the sales manager who drives for volume in terms of units or pounds and sacrifices profit by overwilling reduction of prices; the engineer who pursues quality without consideration of costs; the researcher who wants to hold the new product in the laboratory until all possible refinements are effected; and the specialist in operations research who prefers to work on problems responsive to his techniques rather than more important though less structured problems. The general manager, without robbing the essential specialist of his incentive to sustain and increase his technical competence, must find a way to interest the specialist in the importance of the interfunctional mission to which his specialty is being applied.

In performing the task of reconciling the needs and demands of one set of specialists with those of all the others, the general manager is in some ways at a disadvantage. The rise of specialism, valuable and necessary as it has been, has been accompanied by an unnecessary and unjustifiable decline in the attractiveness of the role of the generalist. This appears to have several origins other than the natural conviction of the specialist that everything outside his area is relatively trivial. Most important, the role of the generalist appears to be without substance, to elude rigorous theory and disciplined research. Humbug, folklore, ignorance, and manipulation of power have indeed proved poor substitutes for a systematic, researchable, reasoned approach to the many duties of general management. Where general management has been well-intentioned and skillful, it has often seemed the intuitive projection of personal magnetic powers, not really understood and certainly not capable of direct perpetuation. Where fear and power were the principal tools of top management, the function would not be much respected. Theories of general management have consisted of exhortations to plan, organize, integrate, and measure, for example, with little being communicated on how to perform these grand functions in concrete situations.

General management may not have deserved the kind of respect accorded to more specific disciplines. Certainly the difficulties in the way of making it a true discipline are many. But the general manager need not on that account think badly of his function. He is accorded the power to hire and fire specialists, to use them or not as he sees fit, and to direct their activities. The status, prestige, and compensation accorded to him are evidence that not everyone agrees with the specialist's denigration of the intellectual substance of the generalist's domain.

The successful management of specialized functions requires first that the generalist relinquish his own pride of specialty. This has an important price. It alienates him from his former associates who may believe, like some of their counterparts in the university, that only second-rate disciplinarians would undertake roles for which no rigorous preparation exists and whose future is even more uncertain. It virtually ensures that he will generally become obsolete in his specialty, for, as we have seen, general management provides little time for hobbies.

The generalist must himself take the pride in his own function—which only knowledge of what it is can sustain, once his satisfactions with status and compensation become routine. The coordinating function that balances the roles and needs of specialties against the requirements of the mission of a total enterprise has long been known to be essential. Chester Barnard once asserted what no one has effectively contradicted—namely, that the quality of coordination in an organization is the most essential determinant of its survival. The power of group effort is not felt until differences in point of view are recognized and dealt with and the contributions of specialists in a planned division of labor have been fitted together.

The generalist has another important professional function which should add dignity to rather than detract from his role. He is responsible for the translation of specialized knowledge into successful action. In performing this responsibility he enables the specialist to fulfill his role. He necessarily takes responsibility for the impact of action upon his company and its markets.

It is also the generalist's function to add humane concern not only to the activities of his organization but to its relationship to its communities. His assignment requires him to conceive of the technology and specialized systems of his company's business operations as ultimately a human problem. If it is his function to preside over specialized expertness being combined into effective products and services, he has the satisfaction of making it finally worthwhile.

"The managerial life," as David Lilienthal said his whole life's experience had taught him, "is the broadest, the most demanding, by all odds the most comprehensive and the most subtle of all human activities. And the most crucial."

The skills of the generalist, made necessary by his responsibilities and by the problems arising from rampant specialism, arise naturally from the point of view and perspective essential to his assignment. The generalist's loyalty is to no function or process but to the most effective combination of talent applicable to the successive missions of his organization. He must be able to identify the kinds of specialists he most needs, for he cannot afford them all. He must recognize the conflict between functional needs and organizational needs. He must permit the continuous development of functional skills and the survival of the values attending those skills. At the same time he must provide tangible incentive for the development in specialists of tolerance for other specialists and for the constraints and opportunities imposed by organizational purposes. He must turn specialists to the interfunctional task; to do this he must find a way to make organizational goals more attractive than departmental goals.

The generalist above all cannot allow himself to be intimidated by the language, demeanor, and organizational insensitivity of his highly educated subordinates. He must not pretend to understand what he does not, and he should persist in his questioning until he is satisfied. Without being suspicious of his departments' plans and purposes, he can continually inquire into the relevance of departmental aspirations and objectives to those of the total organization. To do this, he must become familiar with both. Ultimately, he aims to lead a team of specialists who are competent in the technical expertise they are expected to accumulate but who are also committed to the goals and purposes of the organization. Conflicts, misunderstandings, and disappointments that result from the shifting role of functions as circumstances change should have as large a place on the agenda of management discussions as less important but more conventional topics.

The successful generalist survives and succeeds in a specialized world by virtue of his management skills rather than his technical knowledge. If he makes his specialists into managers as well, the inevitable differences in point of view become negotiable. To do this he must have not only a clear but a communicable concept of what his firm's evolving needs for functional expertness are to be.

NEED FOR A CONCEPT

If the real importance of the generalist has been undervalued and if too little research and education have gone into the systematic preparation of generalists, this must have taken place because the relation between the general manager and the technical manager is too little understood. If, in view of our empirical experience with the importance of general management, we understand too little about it, this must be because we do not have a way of viewing the process which permits agreement on language, systematic research, and experimental inquiry into better and less good ways of conducting it. Such indeed has been the case.

It is perfectly clear that, though the world has seen much good general management, we need a better conceptual scheme for understanding it and better ways of deliberately perpetuating it. Both require at least a simple theory of what effective general management entails. The problems that have caused the practice of management to remain primarily intuitive are obvious. Given the unruly variety of business activity, the instability of chosen courses of action resulting from competitive moves and countermoves, and the need for flexibility, we encounter at once the staggering improbability of being able to specify a complete theory of general management appropriate to all industry and commerce. We know we cannot expect a series of formulas to regulate the long-term conduct over time of a dynamic enterprise. On the other hand, we also know much about the limitations of intuition, and we appreciate the urgent and obvious need for planning if we are to achieve leadership in any competition in which we engage. Leadership in an industry cannot be achieved or sustained forever by brilliant improvisation or by sheer mass.

As a means of reducing the four-faceted responsibility of the general manager to more reasonable proportions, to subject it to more objective research and evaluation, and to bring within reach of more well-endowed people the skills it demands, we propose here a simple practitioner's theory. To be useful this theory must embrace the whole business. It must permit impartiality with respect to the importance of individual functions. It must insist on the worth of the specialized functions, yet subordinate them dispassionately to the principal objectives of the business. It must define the general manager's role in such a way as to allow delegation of much of the general management responsibility to other managers without loss of definition or clarity.

Our theory begins with the simple proposition that every business organization, every subunit of organization, and even every individual should have a clearly defined set of purposes or goals which keeps it moving in a deliberately chosen direction and prevents its drifting in undesired directions. The primary function of the general manager, over time, is supervision of the continuous process of determining the nature of the enterprise and setting, revising, and attempting to achieve its goals. If this definition of the manager's central function could be brought alive and made to seem real to all the staff specialists whose best efforts are required to determine the potential return for all the best available alternatives, the conflict between them and the senior executive who must finally make or ratify the goal-setting decision will be resolved, more often than it is now, in a productive conversation free of negative and wasteful emotion.

In the next chapter we shall attempt to sketch how in practice the simple determination to give the highest priority to goal-setting may result in a durable but flexible concept of the company's corporate strategy. We shall see how "corporate strategy" can be used to guide over a long period of time the development of the company's ability to achieve superior results without depriving it of the capability for quick response to changing conditions. How to define, decide, and put into effect a conscious strategy will then take precedence over and lend order to the four-fold functions of general management which we enumerated earlier.

We should expect neither too much nor too little of this idea. It is less new than untried. We propose the substitution of the instinctive practice of experienced natural business leaders by a consciously decided and articulated program to which the whole organization can give heed. To lift the intuitive sense of what the business is and is becoming to the level of articulateness is not so big a step, but it may be essential to keeping strategy current, exposing it to question, and making it available for dramatization and publication to shareholders, employees, and customers. Members of these groups are as susceptible as anyone to any impression that a company knows what it is doing, and they are likely to repay clarification with confidence. To state and dramatize the purpose of a company and as much as is known or prudent to disclose of its plans for achievement of these purposes is a crucial step in tightening the bonds uniting the company to its most important constituencies.

The clarification of corporate purpose, once the conflicts attending the process are resolved, is strikingly useful in resolving the conflicts that arise during the course of concerted action to achieve those purposes. Like individuals, line and staff groups aware of common goals and without suspicion of each others' purposes are unlikely to be at loggerheads about means of implementation. A manager who is sure that his subordinates know what their targets are is more likely than he otherwise would be to let them experiment with new methods promising better results than do existing routines.

In advanced industries and markets, a considerable lead time is required to develop proprietary products, to devise systems services of original importance, to establish a commanding position in a market or market segment, and to strengthen the organizational capability to attain and maintain preeminence. If leadership is to be anything but stabs in the dark and strokes of luck, it follows that plans for such outcomes must be made in advance. To focus organizational energy and assets, purpose must be predetermined and a relationship between development projects established which economizes effort and consolidates both the firm's advantage over its rivals and its promotable claims to uniqueness and preeminence.

The apparently simple step of stating in terms broad enough to be stimulating rather than restrictive yet concrete enough to exclude irrelevant endeavors makes possible holding before an organization a vision of what it might accomplish and what the rewards of successful effort will be. The way is opened to dispel the apathy that makes much organized effort lackluster and unsatisfying, to create commitment and dedication in its place. Goals clear enough to attract people willing to devote their loyalty to such goals and to turn away others are a powerful force in shaping the character and capability of an organization. An organization of uncommitted people is at worst parasitic and at best a bore for all its members.

The generalist needs a clear decision about organization purposes in order to know what specialists he needs and how to coordinate their output. He needs deliberately decided strategy in order to know the organization structure that will deploy and relate specialties most effectively for the organization purposes to be served. He needs clearly articulated corporate purposes in order to provide the incentive and control systems that will reward specialist contributions in proportion to their organizational value.

Much difficulty intervenes, as we shall see, between the determination to clarify purpose and the realization of all these benefits. The path must not be easy to follow, for fewer general managers actually take it than say they intend to.

The Concept of
Corporate Strategy

WITH THE PROSPECT that it may prove the general manager's most important stock in trade, the substance of his own expertness, and the means for integrating the work of his specialized assistants, we come now to the concept of corporate strategy itself. It is the purpose of this chapter to make clear the idea of corporate strategy, the uses and limitations of the concept, the criteria that may be used to test the soundness and continuing utility of a strategy, and the problems of evaluation that we should expect to encounter in considering strategic alternatives.

DEFINITION

Our use of the term "corporate strategy" comprises more than the usual military connotations of this term.

26

For the military, *strategy* is most simply the science and art of employing a nation's armed strength to secure goals prescribed by the nation's leaders. *Tactics,* a term brought to mind whenever *strategy* is used in the military sense, denotes the less broad science and art of disposing and maneuvering armed forces against the enemy. Thus, in this use strategy neither includes the choice of goals nor the detailed plans or action for achieving them. It appears to be the marshalling of resources which will provide the best opportunity for subsequent tactics to be effective.

When we switch from warfare to business, we find that the lines separating goals and objectives, the grand designs for securing and deploying resources appropriate to those goals, the more specific policies guiding use of these resources, and the programs guided by policies carried out in the field of action become even harder to keep clear than to maintain the difference between strategy and tactics in warfare. Business is far more various and disorderly—though almost always less deadly—than warfare. That objectives and goals are usually multiple and various and that they are usually arranged in a hierarchy from something very lofty or broad to something mundane or specific, complicate our approach to definition.

An important objective of a business may appear, for example, in the form of seeking and maintaining first place in research, development, sales, and profits in the information-processing business. Another may be making the company a stimulating place to work. Still another objective may be to have a constantly better safety record, or to have 12 percent of the worker population black.

Policy is just as much an accordion-like word as is *objective*. If a policy is a guide to action serving an objective, then it in turn can be an objective served by more specific policy. It may be a company's policy to omit or relax testing procedures for prospective employees from disadvantaged minorities in order to attain its goal of 12 percent black employees, but, for the corporate personnel director enforcing policy throughout a widespread corporation, getting these testing procedures amended may be a goal in itself. Objectives thus can be all-encompassing or specific. In descending hierarchical order objectives can be policies for reaching higher goals. Similarly, a program of action implementing policy can also be for subdivisions of organization both objective and policy. Under a policy allowing him the choice, the janitor may order supplies to keep his new building clean. Filling this order and keeping this business may be a major objective of his small supplier. Under some circumstances an objective once achieved becomes policy, and a policy thoroughly institutionalized becomes routine action.

That action, policy, and purpose change roles so readily has led us to concentrate at the top of the hierarchy of corporate objectives, to sidestep the problem of drawing distinctions between objectives, policy, and programs of action, and to avoid speaking of single or functional strategies except as aspects of total corporate strategy. For us *corporate strategy is the pattern of major objectives, purposes, or goals and essential policies and plans for achieving those goals, stated in such a way as to define what business the company is in or is to be in and the kind of company it is or is to be.* In a changing world it is a way of expressing a persistent concept of the business so as to exclude some possible new activities and suggest entry into others. What a man does determines and reveals over time what he is and why he does it. So it is with a company.

Why our definition of strategy includes the choice of

purpose as well as the essential policy-level means for achieving it will become more clear as we explore the interdependence of purposes, policies, and organized action in particular situations. In the meantime, we will not argue further whether the term should include the selection of goals or denote only the deployment of resources marshalled in pursuit of these goals. We are less concerned with exactness of language than we might be if development of theory were our first objective.

It is to us a matter of indifference. Little confusion results so long as we make clear what we are doing. It is important only to remember that the choice of goals and the formulation of policy cannot in any case be separate decisions. The Stanford Research Institute takes a different path from ours when it equates strategy with the ways in which the firm, reacting to its environment, deploys its principal resources and marshals its main efforts in pursuit of its purpose. Alfred Chandler, in *Strategy and Structure,* takes the direction we favor when he called strategy ". . . the determination of the basic long-term goals and objectives of an enterprise, and the adoption of courses of action and allocation of resources necessary for carrying out these goals."[1] The reader should make his own choice.

A more important effort to subdivide the idea of strategy seeks to segregate those aspects that are enduring and unchanging over relatively long periods of time from those that are necessarily more responsive to changes in the marketplace and the pressures of other environmental forces. The strategic decision is concerned with the long-term development of the enterprise. It necessarily projects continuously into the future. The central character of a

---

[1]Alfred D. Chandler, Jr., *Strategy and Structure: Chapters in the History of the Industrial Enterprise* (Cambridge, Mass.: The M.I.T. Press, 1962), p. 13.

business organization and the individuality it has for its members and its various publics may, in the instance of mature and highly developed corporations, be determined with some clarity.

Thus, the "personality" of firms like Polaroid, Xerox, Control Data, IBM, IT&T, LTV, and General Motors clearly reflects aspects of company or management intent that are manifested only partially in such activities as research expenditures, choice of product line, and the recruitment and development of organization members. It would be likely to persist through substantial changes in the allocation of resources and in product policy, in part because the basic determinants of organization character would tend to prevent sharp discontinuity. The central character of *The New York Times* is likely to be unchanged, even if the services it offers are altered drastically in the direction of increased emphasis on its news service or on the development of other outlets for its news-processing capacity. In this view, the basic character of an enterprise and the core of its special competence would be considered separately from the manifestation of these long-range characteristics in changing product lines, markets, and policies designed to make activities profitable from year to year.

Our primary interest in isolating the need for strategic decision in concrete instances and in determining the most satisfactory pattern of goals and policies makes further refinement of definition or defense of our own preference of little importance. The practicing manager will wish to develop the definition presented here in directions which are useful to him. But before we proceed to clarification by application, we should comment on the terms in which strategy is usually expressed.

A complete summary statement of strategy will in fact say less about what the word means than it does about the company involved. First, it will define products in terms more functional than literal, saying what they do rather than what they are made of. At the same time, unless it is by design a true conglomerate, it will designate clearly the markets and market segments for which products are now or will be designed, and the channels through which these markets will be reached. The means by which the operation is to be financed will be specified, as will the emphasis to be placed on safety of capital versus income return. Usually profit objectives will be stated in terms of earnings per share, return on investment, or return on shareholder equity or some combination of these. Finally, the size and kind of organization which is to be the medium of achievement will be described. It is, of course, more important that the identification of strategy capture the present and projected character of the organization than that it elaborate the categories of purposes just cited.

Some examples of strategy that have been consciously or intuitively determined by the presidents of real companies may make this concept more clear. In examining these illustrations, three points should be kept in mind. First, the conclusion that the strategy is as stated is the writer's deduction from field studies conducted in the companies at a definite period in time. Second, since strategy usually changes over time, either through erosion of purpose or through conscious redirection by management, these statements are probably not accurate statements of current strategy. Thirdly, so persistent is the specialist or functional point of view, members of the managements of these companies and analysts of the cases would probably each restate the strategy reported here to reflect an emphasis important to him. The objective accuracy of the following statements thus may be arguable in detail. For the companies you recognize, the statements are almost certainly out of date. But they will illustrate what we mean by strategy and offer you an opportunity to put down a parallel statement for your own company.

The Continental Watchmakers Company is a Swiss firm (its name we have disguised) which has found for itself a unique and profitable position among its competitors. Analysis of a case study[2] permits us to say:

It is Mr. Keller's present plan to produce watches of the highest quality—in a price range between the hand-made ultraexclusive level and Omega and Rolex. He aims to distribute his watches to all markets of the free world via exclusive wholesale agents and carefully chosen retailers, who are expected to convince customers of the particular value of the product. His growth of about 10% per year is not geared to demand but is deliberately restricted to the productivity of available skilled labor, and to his recognition of cyclical fluctuations in the industry. He aims to maintain within the rules of the industry a stable organization of highly skilled, fully trained workers and a management organization of some breadth, but he apparently wishes to retain personal direction over marketing and a close familiarity with the whole organization.

This strategy is very simple but it distinguishes the product of the company from every other wristwatch in the world. It sustains a steady growth by enabling the loyal retailer to offer a discriminating customer a watch

---

[2]For the text of this case, see E. P. Learned, C. R. Christensen, and K. R. Andrews, *Problems of General Management-Business Policy* (Homewood, Ill.: Richard D. Irwin, Inc., 1961), p. 88.

that can be claimed to be better than an Omega but less expensive than a Patek-Philippe.

Of a very different company, Crown Cork and Seal, we could say, as of the time our case study was completed, the following:[3]

Crown Cork and Seal aims to be a stripped-down and increasingly profitable manufacturer of specialty high-margin rigid containers for hard-to-hold applications (aerosol products and beer) and to maintain its position in bottling machinery and crowns. Its domestic growth will come from increasing the number of geographically decentralized small plants equipped and located to provide fast delivery at low transportation cost and to secure 20 to 40% of each local market. Customer service is led by a technically trained sales force alert to customer needs and by a technical "research" and manufacturing engineering organization which is solving current customer process and packing problems rather than doing basic research. Its current investment in innovation is kept small, but an aggressive marketing and a flexible manufacturing organization are alert to promote advances pioneered by major suppliers and competitors. Domestic operations are intended to be the stable base from which the company can expand internationally. The developing countries to which crown manufacture has already been introduced are expected to be the company's major growth opportunity in containers. Operations will be financed through retained earnings and full use of debt capacity and are expected to return 25¢ additional profit per share per year. The organization will reward drive, energy, and accomplishment and accept rapid turnover in management ranks whenever results fall below expectations.

---

[3]For the text of this case, see E. P. Learned, C. R. Christensen, K. R. Andrews, and W. D. Guth, *Business Policy: Text and Cases* (rev. ed.; Homewood, Ill.: Richard D. Irwin, Inc., 1969), p. 353.

Of Heublein, Inc., now much larger and diversified than when we first studied it in 1965,[4] just before it acquired Hamm's brewery, we once said:

Heublein aims to market in the U.S. and via franchise overseas a wide variety of high margin, high quality consumer products concentrated in the liquor and food business, especially bottled cocktails, vodka, and other special-use and distinctive beverages and specialty convenience foods, addressed to a relatively prosperous, young-adult market and returning over 15% of equity after taxes. With emphasis on the techniques of consumer goods marketing (brand promotion, wide distribution, product representation in more than one price segment, and very substantial off-beat advertising directed closely to its growing audience) Heublein intends to make Smirnoff the number one liquor brand worldwide and to maintain a sales growth of 10% a year worldwide via internal growth or acquisitions or both. Its manufacturing policy rather than full integration is in liquor to redistill only to bring purchased spirits up to high quality standards. It aims to finance its internal growth through the use of debt and its considerable cash flow and to use its favorable price earnings ratio for acquisitions. Both its liquor and food distribution are intended to secure distributor support through advertising and concern for the distributor's profit.

To move on to a company often called a conglomerate, but one which maintains that there is a relationship among its many activities, the Litton cases, completed in 1967,[5] enable one to state the company's strategy thus:

With the objective of building a highly profitable and long lasting major corporation growing at a regulated, striking,

----

[4]For the text of this case, see Learned, Christensen, Andrews, and Guth, *ibid.,* p. 281.

[5]For text, see Learned, Christensen, Andrews, and Guth, *ibid,* p. 808.

but unspecified rate (50% from internal expansion, 50% by acquisition), Litton aims to engage in widely-diversified activities unified by some origin or connection with advanced electronics and beyond that the "concept of converting to practicable and marketable uses the technological developments of the industrial revolution." Among its purposes are a profitable balance between commercial and military electronic products, the use of acquisitions to capitalize its price-earnings multiple, the expansion of the separate units of the company as well as the integration into systems of some of their products and services. Rather than define its business in terms of product line and markets, it seeks to provide a loosely federalized structure in which the units are themselves urged to grow and diversify. This structure is intended to be made effective by a deliberately nurtured atmosphere stressing creativity, innovation, originality, through such processes as opportunity generation and review, informality of organization and communication, dependence on face-to-face communication and telephone calls in lieu of memos and written policies, all controlled by a small corporate staff aware of divisional performance, quick to send help when trouble occurs, slow to prescribe procedure or uniformity, and alert to systems combinations of cross-divisional technical capabilities.

A few years ago case studies completed at Textron[6] seem to reveal this strategy which stresses the separateness rather than the convergence of the divisional activities:

With the aim of being a pure conglomerate, with no part of its original textile business left and with no principal division or product, and with no more than 10% of its net worth invested in any single business, Textron aims to build a multi-market, multi-billion dollar manufacturing company

---

[6]These cases are published in looseleaf form by the Intercollegiate Case Clearing House, Boston, Mass. 02163.

primarily through internal growth and secondarily henceforth through acquisitions. Each division of the company is intended to be the soundest possible performer in its field—usually some aspect of low-technology manufacturing operations, doing between $20 and $250 million in sales. Each division is encouraged to conduct its own research and development and to expand its product line under a broad definition of its business. With the objective of earning 8% pre-tax on sales and 20% on stockholders' equity, the company will sell off companies that cannot be brought up to the latter standard. Textron aims to administer this growing organization with a very small corporate headquarters (fewer than 100 people, mostly line managers and clerical personnel) and a policy manual of less than 25 pages with very close control of cash and capital expenditures and great autonomy in all other matters. A net worth incentive program, a policy of no promotion to corporate levels from divisional ranks, a newly instituted management development program, and an important role for face-to-face communication of division presidents with their group vice presidents are all designed to keep division performance constantly improving.

Companies seldom formulate and publish as complete a statement as we have just illustrated, usually because conscious planning is not carried far enough to achieve the agreement or clarification which publication presumes. But every company has a strategy, imperfect and implicit as it may be. In the absence of explicit statements, the observer may deduce from operations what the goals and policies are, on the assumption that all normal human behavior is purposeful. At the same time the fact that every organization has some kind of strategy does not mean that conscious planning always exists. The *current* strategy of a company may almost always be deduced from its behavior, but a strategy for a *future* of changed circumstance may not always be distinguishable from performance in the present.

Corporate strategy has two equally important aspects, interrelated in life but separated to the extent practicable here in our study of the concept. The first of these is formulation; the second is implementation. Deciding what strategy should be is, at least ideally, a rational undertaking. Its principal subactivities include identifying opportunities and threats in the company's environment and attaching some estimate of risk to the discernible alternatives. Before a choice can be made, the company's strengths and weaknesses must be appraised. Its actual or potential capacity to take advantage of perceived market needs or to cope with attendant risks must be estimated as objectively as possible. The strategic alternative which results from a matching of opportunity and corporate capability at an acceptable level of risk is what we may call an *economic strategy*.

The process described thus far assumes that the strategist is analytically objective in estimating the relative capacity of his company and the opportunity he sees or anticipates in developing markets. The extent to which he wishes to undertake low or high risk presumably depends on his profit objective. The higher he sets the latter, the more willing he must be to assume a correspondingly high risk that the market opportunity he sees will not develop or that the corporate competence required to excel in competition will not be forthcoming.

So far we have described the intellectual processes of ascertaining what a company *might do* in terms of environmental opportunity, of deciding what it *can do* in terms of ability and power, and of bringing these two considerations together in optimal equilibrium. The determination of strategy also requires consideration of what alternative is preferred by the chief executive and perhaps by his immediate associates as well, quite apart from economic considerations. Personal values, aspirations, and ideals do, and in our judgment quite properly should, influence the final choice of purposes. Thus, what the executives of a company *want to do* must be brought into the strategic decision.

Finally, strategic choice has an ethical aspect—a fact much more dramatically illustrated in some industries than in others. Just as alternatives may be ordered in terms of the degree of risk that they entail, so may they be examined against the standards of responsibility that the strategist elects. Some alternatives may seem to the executive considering them more attractive than others when the public good or service to society is considered. What a company *should do* thus appears as a fourth element of the fateful decision we have called strategic.

The ability to identify the four components of strategy —(1) market opportunity, (2) corporate competence and resources, (3) personal values and aspirations, and (4) acknowledged obligations to segments of society other than the stockholders—is nothing compared to the art of reconciling their implications in a final choice of purpose. Taken by itself, each consideration might lead in a different direction.

For example, the manager of a radio station that is declining in ratings and income may decide that in his community the teenage clientele is his best market, especially given the programming practices of competing stations. His program directors, announcers, and advertising salesmen are experienced, however, only in providing a mixture of news, music, and commercials addressed to the adult commuter-motorist, with housewife fare broadcast between rush hours. The manager may hate rock-and-roll music and commercials addressed to the skin problems of adolescents, and his staff may have no real rapport with younger listeners. He may believe that the franchise granted his station to make profit-making use of a publicly owned frequency as well as the policies of the Federal Communications Commission obligate him to some degree of public service more substantial than airing rock and roll.

Something will have to give before a unified strategy can be achieved out of this divergence. At first glance it appears that making a conventional rock approach to teenagers is out, unless his own personal taste and sense of responsibility are to be wholly ignored. Some innovations will be required to end the impasse—either a new approach to teenage listeners or more successful programming for the audience preferred. He might possibly originate a classical concert, news, and public affairs station, defying his original definition of the "best market" and counting on uniqueness and specialized commercials to sustain him. A pioneering reconciliation of some sort is required, for the conventional alternatives in radio programming are inadequate for this problem. Furthermore, the balance finally struck must be adaptable to further changes in the community environment. Since his competitors may shift their own station strategies in reaction to his or in pursuit of ideas of their own, he may have to develop a series of possibilities for future change as vacuums form in market segments in his listening area. In any event, he must make much more sophisticated decisions than the initial ones cited here, that the best market is for teenagers and the kind of station should follow from a conventional idea of what appeals to them.

At a more complex level, a large company engaged in

the worldwide mining and transportation of ores, the reduction of these ores to a metal, and the fabrication of the metal into intermediate and finished goods may find its profits eroded by such problems as overcapacity or price dominance by a larger competitor. It may face an abundance of opportunities, in sharp contrast to the radio station. The alternatives providing highest profit as usual do not match at all with the skills and strengths of the company, for ordinarily high returns attend either a protected opportunity hard to get at or original and unusual capabilities. The location among all the vague possibilities of a new venture optimizing opportunity, corporate capability, and targeted return must lead to a redefinition of opportunity, an extension of capability perhaps by acquisition—a decision influenced both by the preferences of the executives who must make the decision and their satisfaction or lack of it with the social value of the alternative under scrutiny. The difficulties of putting together the results of our examination of the categories of decision essential to a balanced outcome will surely lead to a reconsideration of restructuring the original business for greater profit. Diversification is often an illusory diversion from the opportunities a company is best able to capitalize.

• The implementation of strategy is comprised of a series of subactivities which are primarily administrative. Once purpose is determined, then the resources of a company must be mobilized to accomplish it. An organizational structure that is appropriate for the efficient performance of the required tasks must be made effective by information systems and relationships permitting coordination of subdivided activities. The organizational processes of performance measurement, compensation, management development—all of them enmeshed in systems of incentives and controls—must be directed toward the kind of behavior required by organizational purpose. The role of personal leadership is important and sometimes decisive in the accomplishment of strategy. Since effective implementation can make a sound strategic decision ineffective or a debatable choice thoroughly successful, it is as important to examine the processes of implementation as to weigh the advantages of the available strategic alternatives. The accompanying diagram may be helpful in visualizing the concept of corporate strategy.

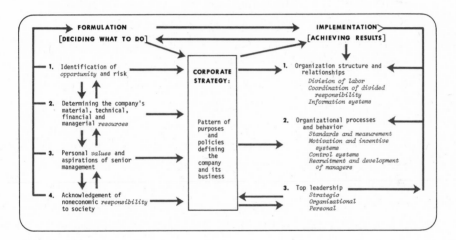

THE FUNCTIONS OF STRATEGY

It is relatively rare, although in substantial organizations less and less so, to encounter the conscious attention to strategy which our definition suggests is appropriate. The many reasons need not detain us now. At the moment, we should consider whether the advantages of a consciously considered strategy are worth the effort it obviously requires. Four considerations suggest an affirmative answer. These are the inadequacy of stating goals only in terms of maximum profit, the necessity for planning ahead

in undertakings with long lead times, the need for influencing rather than merely responding to environmental
change, and the utility of setting visible goals as the ful-
crum of cooperation and an inspiration to organizational
effort.

The age-old assertion that the only true purpose of
business is profit is no substitute for a more detailed program. To specify how much profit in terms of "as much as
possible" leaves unanswered questions about how it is to be
made and whether any restraints are to be observed in the
quest. The extent to which present profits will be forgone to
prepare for larger profits at a later time is unspecified. The
desirability of profit, like that of survival, good health,
and growth, does not make it a magnetic pole establishing
a directed course among many alternatives.

In an era of rapid change and intense interindustry and
intercompany competition, improvisation, however brilliant, cannot suffice as a company's sole weapon against
the negative effects of change. The range of activities
planned in advance is generally wider than that determin-
able on the spur of the moment. Many moves, because
they require long preparation, cannot be made at all without forward planning. When new product development
requires years and a new distribution network may cost
millions of dollars, purpose must necessarily be considered in detail well in advance of investment.

Colorful intuitive leadership may seem to render conscious planning unnecessary. For example, the elder Mr.
Baker of Baker Metal and Foil[7] repeatedly confounded
his subordinates by buying plants and equipment on the
spur of the moment. He planned his moves in the solitude

---

[7] See G. A. Smith and C. R. Christensen, *Policy Formulation and Administration* (rev. ed.; Homewood, Ill.: Richard D. Irwin, Inc., 1955),
p. 453.

of his study during the early hours of the morning, and he doubtless reached a clear decision in his own mind about where he wanted to go. His vision was responsible for his company's status as a leader in its industry. But had he been able to articulate his goals, his associates—relieved of the frustration occasioned by continued chaos—could have more easily performed the financial planning to make them feasible. The forward look which Mr. Baker took in solitude did not in itself constitute the formulation of a coherent strategy that would permit his organization to know what he was up to and what was required of them.

Planned purpose can affect and change the character of future developments which otherwise might endanger even the healthiest organization. Reliance upon adaptation alone leaves the company at the mercy of the strongest currents. Innovation, and the creativity which supports it, can enable a company to carve out its own future rather than simply to depend on favorable circumstances. But such a course requires predetermination of what must be done. Thus, at least one manufacturer of small radios and another of camera equipment, apparently about to be overwhelmed by Japanese imports, stemmed the tide and reversed a trend by a program comprising cost reduction, product restyling, and improved marketing, all of which took time and predetermined purpose to perfect.

From the point of view of implementation, the most important function of strategy is to serve as the focus of organizational effort, as the object of commitment, and as the source of constructive motivation and self-control in the organization itself. We shall have ample opportunity to see later that it it a common understanding of the goals to be served and a widespread acceptance of their importance, persisting through the inevitable distortions of individual and departmental needs, that are the soundest bases of cooperative action.

THE LIMITATIONS OF STRATEGY

These claims regarding the value of formulating a strategy, which began to make their appearance in the previous chapter, are stated as ideas to be examined and tested, for the practice is not without its limitations. One objection sometimes voiced is that strategy involves planning, and that planning ahead is really not possible. With increasing complexity and an accelerating rate of change, it grows more and more difficult to predict the future in detail. Long-range plans cannot be detailed quantitatively with much confidence. Accuracy in forecasting is impossible. Planning takes time and sometimes formal planning becomes elaborate and frustrating. These complaints are not real limitations, however, for strategy does not require more knowledge of the future or more time than we have. The extent to which a variety of alternatives is studied in advance reduces the possibility of surprise and permits the preparation of alternative plans for a range of possibilities. The more uncertain the future, in fact, the more necessary it is to contemplate what can happen and what is likely to happen and to assign probabilities to the imaginable possibilities.

A more serious limitation is that overdedication to plan may result in lost opportunity. The rise of research expenditures and the impossibility of knowing in advance what research will bring forth often lead opponents of planning to say with some justice that maintenance of flexibility to take advantage of unanticipated opportunity is more important than commitment to fixed plans over long time periods. One must admit at once that the determination of strategy must not be so rigid that unexpected opportunity cannot be considered. But it is possible to conceive of strategy as being firm and influential without its being cast in concrete. We shall ultimately be able to conceive of strategy as performing all that we ask of it without ever becoming finally solidified. To accommodate uncertainty and to preserve flexibility are not the easiest activities in the world, but a strategy formulated without regard for these necessities would indeed be folly. What is needed is the concept of a moving balance among the considerations on which strategy is based, the concept of a strategy that progressively evolves in the direction of improving the match between the company's resources and the opportunities in its environment. Finally, to design a strategy that is *optimal* is a challenge to insight and intelligence which simply lies beyond the capacity of many an effective operator. The skill required in the use of an idea may indeed be a limitation to its usefulness.

A third set of limitations and problems which requires us to say at once that the concept of strategy is no panacea is the inevitability of conflict between corporate and departmental goals and between organizational and personal goals. We shall have more to say about these impediments to effective implementation at a later time. In the meantime, we must accept as a fact of life that whenever different values produce different opinions in a top management group about how its company should develop, a clear strategy will not be produced until these differences have been candidly disclosed and accommodated. Furthermore, the most articulate, specific, and persuasive definition of strategy by the president of a company, ratified by the board of directors and promptly emulated by competitors, will never have the same meaning or appeal to all parts of the organization to which it is announced.

To communicate a strategy requires as much trouble and time as to conceive it. Witness George Romney's long attempt to persuade his own people that the small car was the proper niche for American Motors and his successor's ruinous departure from this idea.[8] To adhere to it wisely under the temptations posed by expediency is difficult. To adhere to it blindly when changing circumstance has made it obsolete is no more preferable than thoughtless opportunism. New opportunities, unexpected innovations, sudden emergencies, competitive pressures, and incomplete programming of action required by the strategy selected all constitute real problems in adhering to a plan once it has been made clear.

The advantages of attempting to communicate a clear strategy are not available when valid reasons for secrecy call for remaining closemouthed. A company in the office equipment business may not wish to announce its long-term strategy to acquire a substantial computer manufacturer for fear of inviting competition, prejudicing negotiations, and alarming the Department of Justice. Although the need for secrecy is often exaggerated and sometimes used as a cloak for indecision, it is not usually prudent to make detailed strategy available to competitors. If a company must go out of a business it has been active in for a generation, it may not be possible to communicate this at once to the people involved, who incidentally are probably quite aware of the possibility. But to overlook the need for such a decision because of the impracticality of publishing it is without justification. Nothing in this obvious truth, nor in the corollary that it is unwise to produce for the files long memoranda on all the things a company might do, prevents a chief executive

[8]For case studies of American Motors, see E. P. Learned, C. R. Christensen, K. R. Andrews, and W. D. Guth, *ibid,* p. 60.

or a small group of senior executives from making individual decisions with a master strategy in mind. If it has coherence and is sound, subordinates will sense its presence and be spared the frustrations of random contemplation of alternatives and be motivated by the feeling that the company's leaders know what they are doing.

The limitations of the concept of strategy consist principally then of the inherent *difficulties* of conceiving an original pattern of goals and policies and implementing them wisely. Dealing with these limitations effectively means not abandoning the concept, but learning to use it successfully with reasonable perspective on what is possible. We cannot expect the concept of strategy to be a substitute for judgment or a shortcut to wisdom. It does not in itself point out the course of action to be taken in difficult situations. Nevertheless, it is the strategic decision to which judgment must be applied. Wisdom cannot be brought to a decision that is not recognized as needed. No consideration of the limitations of this idea invalidates the proposition that the essential business and character of an enterprise should be determined well in advance of shifting circumstances. Otherwise, shifting circumstances become the determining factors, and the future of the corporation is no longer within the control of its management.

H. Edward Wrapp, in a well-known article called "Good Managers Don't Make Policy Decisions,"[9] argues persuasively that the art of imprecision is one of the five principal skills of a general manager. (The first three are "Keeping Well Informed," "Focusing Time and Energy," and "Playing the Power Game.") The argument that specific objectives should not be published can easily be con-

---

[9] *Harvard Business Review,* September-October, 1967, pp. 91–99.

fused with the issue whether specific objectives should even be determined. Wrapp's fifth skill, "Muddling with a Purpose," suggests the futility of imposing a total program upon an organization and the wisdom of piecing together the proposals that come to the chief executive that move the company part way toward his objectives. Again the need for the manager to *know his objectives* is in no way diminished by the political problems of getting them accepted. Strategic indecision cannot be defended because the communication of strategy properly formulated and continuously reviewed is either difficult or inadvisable.

CRITERIA FOR EVALUATION

The attempt to identify the actual or optimal strategy for a business firm raises at once the question of how the actual or proposed strategy is to be judged. How are we to know that one strategy is better than another in advance of validation by experience? As is already evident, no infallible indicators are available. A number of important questions can regularly be asked.[10] With practice they will lead to intuitive discriminations.

1. *Is the strategy identifiable and has it been made clear either in words or practice?*

The degree to which attention has been given to the strategic alternatives available to a company is likely to be basic to the soundness of its strategic decision. To cover in empty phrases ("our policy is planned profitable growth in any market we can serve well") an absence of analysis of opportunity or actual determination of corpo-

---

[10]For an earlier statement of most of the criteria discussed here, see Seymour Tilles, "How to Evaluate Corporate Strategy," *Harvard Business Review,* July-August, 1963, p. 111.

rate strength is worse than to remain silent, for it conveys the illusion of a commitment when none has been made. The unstated strategy cannot be tested or contested and is likely therefore to be weak. If it is implicit in the intuition of a strong leader, his organization is likely to be weak and the demands his strategy makes upon it are likely to remain unmet. A strategy must be explicit to be effective and specific enough to require some actions and exclude others.

2. *Does the strategy fully exploit domestic and international environmental opportunity?*

An unqualified yes answer is likely to be rare, even in the instance of global giants like General Motors. But the present and future dimensions of markets can be analyzed without forgetting the limited resources of the planning company in order to outline the requirements of balanced growth and the need for environmental information. The relation between market opportunity and organizational development is a critical one in the design of future plans. Unless growth is incompatible with the resources of an organization or the aspirations of its management, it is likely that a strategy that does not purport to make full use of market opportunity will be weak also in other respects. Vulnerability to competition is increased by lack of interest in market share.

3. *Is the strategy consistent with corporate competence and resources, both present and projected?*

Although additional resources, both financial and managerial, are available to companies with genuine opportunity, the availability of each must be finally determined and programmed along a practicable time scale. The decision of the Wilkinson Sword Company to distribute stainless steel razor blades in the United States must have raised the question whether the company could in effect take yes for an answer from this market—that is, whether its productive capacity could be increased fast enough to fend off the countermoves of large competitors.

○ 4. *Are the major provisions of the strategy and the program of major policies of which it is comprised internally consistent?*

A foolish consistency is the hobgoblin of little minds, and consistency of any kind is certainly not the first qualification of successful corporation presidents. Nonetheless, one advantage of making as specific a statement of strategy as is practicable is the resultant availability of a careful check on coherence, compatibility, and synergy—the state in which the whole can be viewed as greater than the sum of its parts. For example, a manufacturer of chocolate candy who depends for most of his business upon wholesalers should not follow a policy of ignoring them or of dropping all support of their activities and all attention to their complaints. Similarly, two engineers who found a new firm expressly to do development work should not follow a policy of accepting orders that, though highly profitable, in effect turn their company into a large job shop, with the result that unanticipated financial and production problems take all the time that might have gone into development. An examination of any substantial firm will reveal at least some details in which policies pursued by different departments tend to go in different directions. When inconsistency threatens concerted effort to achieve budgeted results within a planned time period, then consistency becomes a vital rather than merely an aesthetic problem.

5. *Is the chosen level of risk feasible in economic and personal terms?*

Strategies vary in the degree of risk willingly undertaken by their designers. For example, the Midway Foods

Company[11] in pursuit of its marketing strategy, deliberately courted disaster in production slowdowns and in erratic behavior of cocoa futures. But the choice was made knowingly and the return, if success were achieved, was likely to be correspondingly great. Temperamentally, the president was willing to live under this pressure and presumably had resources if disaster were to strike. At the other extreme, a company may have such modest growth aspirations that the junior members of its management are unhappy. A more aggressive and ambitious company would be their choice. Although risk cannot always be assessed scientifically, the level at which it is set is, within limits, optional. The riskiness of any future plan should be compatible with the economic resources of the organization and the temperament of the managers concerned.

6. *Is the strategy appropriate to the personal values and aspirations of the key managers?*

Until we consider the relationship of personal values to the choice of strategy, it is not useful to dwell long upon this criterion. But, to cite an extreme case, the deliberate falsification of warehouse receipts to conceal the absence of soybean oil from the tanks which are supposed to contain it would not be an element of competitive strategy to which most of us would like to be committed. A strong attraction to leisure, to cite a less extreme example, is inconsistent with a strategy requiring all-out effort from the senior members of a company. Or if, for example, the president abhors conflict and competition, then it can be predicted that the hard-driving firm of an earlier day will have to change its strategy. Conflict between the personal preferences, aspirations, and goals of the key members of an organization and the plan for its future is a sign of

---

[11]See Learned, Christensen, and Andrews, *op. cit.,* p. 143.

danger and a harbinger of mediocre performance or **fail-ure.**

7. *Is the strategy appropriate to the desired level of contribution to society?*

Closely allied to the value criterion is the ethical criterion. As the professional obligations of business are acknowledged by an increasing number of senior managers, it grows more and more appropriate to ask whether the current strategy of a firm is as socially responsible as it might be. Although it can be argued that filling any economic need contributes to the social good, it is clear that a manufacturer of cigarettes might well consider diversification on grounds other than his fear of future legislation. These days all manufacturers discharging pollutants to air and water and offering offense to eye and ear must rest uneasy.

8. *Does the strategy constitute a clear stimulus to organizational effort and commitment?*

For organizations which aspire not merely to survive but to lead and to generate productive performance in a climate that will encourage the development of competence and the satisfaction of individual needs, the strategy selected should be examined for its inherent attractiveness to the organization. Some undertakings are inherently more likely to gain the commitment of able men of goodwill than others. Given the variety of human preferences, it is risky to illustrate this difference briefly. But currently a company that is vigorously expanding its overseas operations finds that several of its socially conscious young men exhibit more zeal in connection with its work in developing countries than in Europe. Generally speaking, the bolder the choice of goals and the wider the range of human needs they reflect, the more successfully they will appeal to the capable membership of a healthy and energetic organization.

9. *Are there early indications of the responsiveness of markets and market segments to the strategy?*

Results, no matter how long postponed by necessary preparations, are, of course, the most telling indicators of soundness, so long as they are read correctly at the proper time. A strategy may pass with flying colors all the tests so far proposed, and may be in internal consistency and uniqueness an admirable work of art. But if, within a time period made reasonable by the company's resources and the original plan, the strategy does not work, then it must be weak in some way that has escaped attention. Bad luck, faulty implementation, and competitive counter-moves may be more to blame for unsatisfactory results than flaws in design, but the possibility of the latter should not be unduly discounted. Conceiving a strategy that will win the company a unique place in the business community that will give it an enduring concept of it-self, that will harmonize its diverse activities, and that will provide a fit between environmental opportunity and present or potential company strength is an extremely complicated task. We cannot, therefore, expect simple tests of soundness to tell the whole story. But an analytical examination of any company's strategy against the several criteria here suggested will nonetheless give anyone concerned with making, proving, or contributing to corporate planning a good deal to think about.

Problems of Evaluation

The evaluation of strategy is as much an act of judgment as is the original conception, and may be as subject to error. The most common source of difficulty is the mis-evaluation of current results. When results are unsatisfactory, as we have just pointed out, a reexamination of strategy is called for. At the same time, outstandingly good current results are not necessarily evidence that the strategy is sound. For example, the candy manufacturer we have already mentioned made more money from his newly established retail stores just after the war than from the rest of his operations, but these profits were poor evidence that he was doing what he should have been doing. With the end of sugar rationing and the return of a buyers' market, he suddenly went bankrupt. Extrapolation of present performance into the future, overoptimism and complacence, and underestimation of competitive response and of the time required to accommodate to change in demand are often by-products of success. Unusually high profits may blind the unwary manager to impending environmental change. His concern for the future can under no circumstances be safely suspended. Conversely, a high-risk strategy that has failed was not necessarily a mistake, so long as the risk was anticipated and the consequences of failure carefully calculated. In fact, a planning problem confronting a number of diversified companies today is how to encourage their divisions to undertake projects where failure can be afforded but where success, if it comes, will be attended by high profits not available in run-of-the-mill, low-risk activities.

Although the possibility of misinterpreting results is by far the commonest obstacle to accurate evaluation of strategy, the criteria previously outlined suggest immediately some additional difficulties. It is as easy to misevaluate corporate resources and the financial requirements of a new move as to misread the environment for future opportunities. To be overresponsive to industry trends may be as dangerous as to ignore them. For example, if a manufacturer of jeweled-lever watches should switch his production to pin-lever watches because of the success of Timex in the United States and the faster growth rate of inexpensive watches in other countries, his course would not necessarily be correct. The correspondence of the company's strategy with current environmental developments and an overreadiness to adapt may obscure the opportunity for a larger share of a declining market or for growth in profits without a parallel growth in total sales. The already cited decision of American Motors not to follow trends toward big cars in the middle 1950s provides us with an opportunity to examine the strategic alternatives of adapting to, or running counter to, massive current trends in demand.

The intrinsic difficulty of determining and choosing among strategic alternatives leads many companies to do what the rest of the industry is doing rather than to make an independent determination of opportunity and resources. Sometimes the companies of an industry run like sheep all in one direction. The similarity among the strategies, at least in some periods of history, of insurance companies, banks, railroads, and airplane manufacturers may lead one to wonder whether strategic decisions were based upon industry convention or upon independent analysis. Discouragingly often, decisions in the farm equipment, rubber, steel, and automobile businesses raise questions whether the similarity of timing, decision, and reaction to competition constituted independent appraisals of each company's situation, or whether imitation took the place of independent decision. At any rate, the similarity of one company's strategy to that of its competitors does not constitute the soundness which it might at first suggest.

A strategy may manifest an all-too-clear correspondence with the personal values of the founder, owner, or chief executive. Like a correspondence with dominant trends and the strategic decisions of competitors, this may also be unproductive. For example, a personal preference for growth beyond all reasonable expectations may be given undue weight. It should be only one factor among several in any balanced consideration of what is involved in designing strategy. The HMH Publishing Company, which operates *Playboy Magazine* and the Key Clubs, among other enterprises, is dominated by Hugh Hefner's concept of the good life. If his concept changes, as with increasing maturity it may, successive groups of affluent young adult aspiring followers currently for some reason attracted by his present values may turn elsewhere for guidance. (This might be a greater loss to the company, of course, than to society at large.) Too little attention to a corporation's actual competence for growth or diversification is the commonest error of all.

It is thus entirely possible that a strategy may reflect in an exaggerated fashion the values rather than the reasoned decisions of the responsible manager or managers and that imbalance may go undetected. That this may be the case is a reflection of the fact that the entire business community may be dominated by certain beliefs of which one should be wary. A critic of strategy must be at heart enough of a nonconformist to raise questions about generally accepted modes of thought and the conventional thinking which serves as a substitute for original analysis. The timid may not find it prudent to challenge publicly some of the ritual of policy formulation. But even for them it will serve the purposes of criticism to inquire privately into such sacred propositions as the one proclaiming that a company must grow or die or that price-earnings multiples may be sustained only by quarterly increases of earnings per share.

Another canon of management that may engender questionable strategies is the idea that cash funds in excess of reasonable dividend requirements should be reinvested either in revitalization of a company's traditional activities or in mergers and acquisitions that will diversify products and services. Successful operations, a heretic might observe, sometimes bring riches to a company which lacks the capacity to reemploy them. Yet a decision to return to the owners large amounts of capital which the company does not have the competence or desire to put to work is an almost unheard-of development. It is therefore appropriate, particularly in the instance of very successful companies in older and stable industries, to inquire how far strategy reflects a simple desire to put all resources to work rather than a more valid appraisal of investment opportunity in relation to unique corporate strengths. We should not forget to consider an unfashionable, even if ultimately also an untenable alternative— namely, that to keep an already large worldwide corporation within reasonable bounds, a portion of the assets might well be returned to stockholders for investment in other enterprises. The rise of takeover attempts has called attention to the vulnerability of being idly rich.

The identification of opportunity and choice of purpose are such challenging intellectual activities that we should not be surprised to find that persistent problems attend the proper evaluation of strategy. But just as the criteria for evaluation are useful, even if not precise, so the dangers of misevaluation are less menacing if they are recognized. We have noted the inexactness of the concept of strategy, the limits to its usefulness in practice, the problems of making resolute determinations in the face of uncertainty, the necessity for judgment in the evaluation of the soundness of strategy, and the misevaluation into which human error may lead us. None of these alters the fact that a business enterprise guided by a clear sense of purpose rationally arrived at and emotionally ratified by commitment is more likely to have a successful outcome, in terms of profit and social good, than a company whose future is left to guess work and chance. Conscious strategy does not preclude brilliance of improvisation or the welcome consequences of good fortune. Its cost is principally thought and hard work which, though often painful, are seldom fatal.

The Company and Its Environment: Relating Opportunity and Resources

DETERMINATION of a suitable strategy for a company begins in identifying the opportunities and risks in its environment. This chapter is concerned with the identification of a range of strategic alternatives, the narrowing of this range by recognizing the constraints imposed by corporate capability, and the determination of one or more economic strategies at acceptable levels of risk. We shall examine the complexity and variety of the environmental forces which must be considered and the problems of accuracy in assessing company strengths and weaknesses. Economic strategy will be viewed as the match between qualification and opportunity which relates a firm

59

to its environment. We shall attempt, in passing, to categorize the kinds of economic strategies that result from the combination of internal capability and external market needs, and to relate these categories to the normal course of corporate development.

THE NATURE OF THE COMPANY'S ENVIRONMENT

The environment of a company in business, like that of any other organic entity, is the pattern of all the external conditions and influences that affect its life and development. The environmental influences relevant to strategic decision operate in a company's industry, the total business community, its city, its country, and the world. They are technological, economic, social, and political in kind. The corporate strategist is usually at least intuitively aware of these features of the current environment about him. But in all these categories change is taking place at varying rates—fastest in technology, less rapidly in politics. Change in the environment of business necessitates continuous monitoring of a company's definition of its business lest it become inappropriate or even obsolete. Since by definition the formulation of strategy is performed at any one time with the future in mind, the executive must be aware of those aspects of his company's environment which are susceptible to the kind of change that will affect his company's future.

From the point of view of the corporate strategist, technological developments are not only the fastest unfolding but the most far-reaching in extending or contracting opportunity for an established company. They include the discoveries of science, the impact of related product development, and the progress of automation. We see in technical progress a continually accelerating rate of change—with new developments piling up before the implications of yesterday's changes can be assimilated. Industries hitherto protected from obsolescence by stable technologies or by the need for huge capital investment become vulnerable to new processes or to cross-industry competition. Science gives the impetus to change not only in technology but also in all the other aspects of business activity.

To James R. Bright, a student of technological change, seven major areas of advance are apparent.[1] These are as follows:

1. Increased *transportation* capability.
    Mastery of greater distances in less time or cost.
    Movement and operations in space, under seas, and in the arctic regions.
2. Increased mastery of *energy*.
    Availability of greater magnitudes and intensity of power.
    Availability of minute quantities of energy, controlled with increased precision.
    Generation and distribution of power from new sources and by new devices.
    Advances in storage of energy.
    New techniques for large scale transportation of fuels and electric power.
3. Increased ability to extend and control *life and serviceability*.
    Longer life for living things.
    Tolerance of extremes of climate.
    Control of growth.

---

[1] James R. Bright, "Opportunity and Threat in Technological Change," *Harvard Business Review*, November-December, 1963, pp. 76–86.

Greater resistance to accident and illness.

Elimination of undesirable forms of life.

Longer life for perishable foods and other organic products.

Reduced deterioration of physical goods.

4. Increased ability to alter *characteristics of materials*.

New properties for old materials.

Synthetic materials.

Combinations of materials to provide new and unique characteristics.

5. Extension of man's *sensory capabilities*.

Vision, via electronics.

Hearing, as in amplification techniques.

Touch, via power controls.

Power of discrimination, via instrumentation to detect minute quantities and dimensions.

Memory, via recording and duplication.

6. Growing *mechanization of physical activity*.

Production (direct labor, work feeding, materials handling, assembly, testing and inspection, packaging).

Distribution (shipping and receiving, warehousing, carrier loading).

Communications and control (movement of paper and mail, recording and assembly of data).

Extractive industries and construction (earth moving, mining, lumbering, and agriculture).

7. Growing *mechanization of intellectual processes*.

Direction of intricate and extended machine processes.

Information processing.

Problem solving.

The simplest impact upon established strategies of these technical trends is the increase of competition and therefore of risk. Transportation advances make feasible competition from distant geographical areas, as from

Japan, in which the advantages in cost of labor may be declining. The changed characteristics of traditional materials will intensify cross-industry competition, as among types of packaging. Technological obsolescence will overcome products whose physical life is greatly extendable, as when automatic typing supplants the still serviceable electric typewriter. Research and development leading to technically advanced products will make new product introductions costlier and product life shorter. At the same time, margins for conventional products will decline as costs of established materials, products, and services are reduced by technological competition.

The risks dramatized by these technical trends can be offset by the new business opportunities opened up for companies that are technically aggressive rather than defensive. The principal consequence of technological advance for any company is the need either to engage in technical development or to maintain a technical intelligence capability enabling it to follow quickly new developments pioneered by others. The massive efforts of American and Continental Can to keep their technology competitive illustrate at least partially the first of these choices. The choice of Crown Cork and Seal to rely more on bringing advances pioneered by their suppliers and competitors quickly to market exemplifies the second. It is neither practical nor necessary for every company to resolve to be at the frontier of all the technical developments that affect the future success of its products and services. At the same time, it is foolhardy to look away very long from the gaudy parade that technological progress constitutes.

We have observed that the environment of a business can be viewed as consisting of technological, economic, social, and political influences. To turn now from technical to economic developments, we may note that these include important international and domestic trends. The world economy is of course affected in time by all the technological advances already alluded to. Amid the political developments we will come to later, we see extension of the Industrial Revolution to the underdeveloped countries of the world, creating a vast expansion of demand and an unprecedented upward surge in standards of living. The prospect is for continued economic growth, even in those crowded countries where increases in population are offsetting recent economic gains and political instability frustrates economic advance.

Global economic development has been and will continue to be a context friendly to the rise of the international and ultimately the multinational corporation. As these world corporations come into conflict with the nationalistic aspirations of developing nations, the concept of total foreign ownership will give way to various forms of partnerships, increasingly state-owned rather than purely private enterprises. Despite struggles to the contrary, as American industries among others seek protection against imports, the internationalization of competition will necessarily be accompanied by an extension of free trade and probably by the growth of trade between the East and West. If the political scene remains stable, economic development should also remain relatively stable as total activity increases steadily.

On the domestic front, economic trends of interest to the executive seeking future opportunity for his company are illustrated by the increasing affluence of the American public, which increases even as we grow less naive in predicting the early end of poverty. In the affluent sector, demand will move beyond the consumption appropriate to material comfort toward culture, travel, and investment. Markets will be segmented, with increased opportunity for high quality, high margin products and services, and special-purpose-systems combinations of these. Technical developments in real time computer services may lead to new patterns of retailing (with decisions made in the home) and in banking, with its dream of a cashless, checkless society.

At lower economic levels the guaranteed minimum income will almost surely raise the standard of living of underprivileged minority groups. The end of the Vietnam war, if it is not succeeded by other international political troubles, should permit funds to be devoted to the physical and social rehabilitation of inner cities. New relations between the public and private sector in pursuit of economic goals will emerge. The American economy will probably move into the much heralded "postindustrial" society, in which older economic activities like mining, agriculture, manufacturing, and construction will be overtaken by the host of services which will dominate economic activity. The large corporation as an institution will continue to be important, especially in providing complex systems services. Without in any way attempting a complete catalog of economic change now taking place in the world, we may conclude that a company remaining oblivious to those developments relevant to its own sphere of activity is courting decline or extinction.

Without attempting to be any more encyclopedic in the area of social change other than strictly economic, we cannot overlook five major trends which will directly or indirectly affect corporate opportunity. First, changing patterns in work and leisure mean not only somewhat more leisure (for everyone except senior executives and strategic planners) but work which emphasizes slide-rule efficiency less and initiative, creativeness, and variety more. The quest of minority groups for redress of old grievances and for equality will become less insistent only as it is satisfied. Thirdly, changing values will produce effects more subtle but no less important than other trends. The shift of interest from self-interest to the good of society, the growing importance of noneconomic incentives at work, the marked development of individualism and the consequent pluralism of a society responding to technological and economic change, and a growing concern for the quality of our environment and of our national goals will affect the response of the public to what large corporations want to do. Changing values will lead to different expectations of the role business should perform.

Although no radical change in our economic or political system appears to be in the offing—despite the appearance of small revolutionary groups in and around university campuses—a business will be expected to perform its economic mission not so much with efficiency (which will still be necessary) but with sensitivity to its environment. It will eventually be prohibited from directly damaging that environment. Organizations in business and out will be called upon more and more not only to be explicit about their goals but to meet the needs and aspirations of their membership. This will undoubtedly be as true of nonprofit organizations as of corporations. Finally, the rising importance of education, in business and without, will lead to corporations not only providing opportunity for continuing education for their employees but to entry on a large scale in operating and providing systems of products and services for educational institutions. The troubles of firms set back by federal budget cuts in the early years of this movement do not gainsay this prediction.

To turn now to the major political forces of importance to an individual firm, we see such major developments as the apparent stabilization of relations between the United States and Soviet Russia, the emergence of Japan as the third great world power, and the shift in potential conflict away from an East-West communist-capitalist confrontation to a North-South conflict of the less developed and fully developed countries. Change in the role of the United States in the world is undoubtedly overdue; it may mean scaling down our peace-keeping commitments and entering into cooperative schemes with other prosperous nations of economic assistance to the less developed regions of the world. At home we can see in the offing a shift in the role of the federal government away from the direct management of massive social programs to providing objectives, funding, and control for efforts performed by local institutions, public and private, and composite organizations. These bodies perforce will become more interdependent and new institutions reflecting private and public partnerships will emerge.

As suggested earlier in connection with changing values, organized life generally will become more democratic or consultative in all institutions to permit flexibility, variety, and innovation. The regulation of business by government and the impact of national planning on private corporate planning will be important forces to deal with whatever course they take. The extent to which regulation is awkward or repressive may turn on what initiative industry takes in proposing sensible regulation and at what ethical level it pursues its own interests. All these possibilities are illustrative allusions to a changing world.

Because so much of what is changing in the world affects the markets for a company's present products, the prospects for future products, and the success of product and market choices, it is, of course, impossible for us to describe or even to know for all business the relevant characteristics of today's world, to say nothing of tomorrow's. We know that a firm—itself a system—is bound in a variety of interrelationships to other larger systems that comprise its economic, technological, social, and political environment. We may conclude that the changes taking place in these larger systems bode both good and ill for the firm. Change threatens all established strategies and requires the businessman to be alert to the possibility that the opportunity he has seized will expire. At the same time, change brings new opportunity for the application of developed expertness and new market needs which entrepreneurial energy may seek to satisfy. No matter how secure a company's position, then, obsolescence of strategy is a continuous threat. At the same time, new opportunities are emerging everywhere as relative affluence puts unprecedented discretionary income into the hands of consumers in developed countries, and as rising income introduces developing countries to material conveniences.

If environmental developments are destroying and creating business opportunities, advance notice of this fact in specific instances is essential to intelligent planning. Fortunately, the fundamental characteristics of any industry can be determined and the requirements of success can be identified and their implications noted, so that responsive action can be taken. The behavior of competitors, for example, is impossible to conceal completely. It can be appraised for the influence it will have and for the assumptions about the future by which it seems to be determined. The identification of new opportunity or of impending threat therefore depends upon knowing what kind of information is relevant. Surveillance of developments becomes more practicable once the critical elements to look for have been determined.

Surveillance of the Changing Environment

It follows, therefore, despite the staggering difficulty — of foreseeing what is to come or even of recognizing the significance of what is already at work in the total environment of business, that some means must be found for organizing systematic intelligence about the changing nature of those forces that most vitally affect a given company or industry. The conceptual apparatus of special disciplines—economics, anthropology, psychology, sociology, and the like—do not produce balanced appraisals, understandably enough, of environmental developments relevant to business decision. No practical system of concepts for environmental analysis appropriate for business has yet been completed or published.

John D. Glover and his colleagues at the Harvard Business School are at work in developing an approach to the total environment of a business firm as an ecological system.[2] The environmental system is comprised of four subsystems changing quantitatively and qualitatively and evolving in orderly relationships. The first of these is the "Community"—the total population of all the individuals and institutions making up the immediate and intermediate context of a company's activities. The second is the "Culture" in which the firm operates—a combination of values, attitudes, beliefs, concepts, customs, and laws that condition the way people and organizations behave in re-

---

[2]The range of Glover's work is illustrated by the titles of essays published for use in the MBA course entitled Planning in the Business Economy and in earlier years in the Advanced Management Program: "Rise and Fall of Corporations: Challenge and Response"; "Environment: 'Community,' 'Culture,' 'Habitat,' and 'Product' "; "The Changing Environment"; "Innovation and Evaluation of the Environment, Part I: Innovation"; "Innovation and Evaluation of the Environment, Part II: Evaluation"; "Patterns and Trends of Environment Development: The Framework for Corporate Planning."

lation to one another and to the physical universe. The third subsystem is designated "Habitat," the natural and man-made physical setting in which the other components of the total ecological system move and have their being. Finally, we have the "Product" of the environmental systems in which the corporation exists and of which it is a part—the stream of goods and services flowing from the firm through its environment toward being consumed or converted to other products. This scheme provides a way for charting the effects of change in any of the systems and for insuring that the planning process be sufficiently comprehensive to reduce the number of unanticipated consequences.

Although the practical utility of this systems approach in organizing knowledge about a company's changing environment is not yet fully developed or demonstrated, it has the immediate impact of preventing the general manager from thinking either that his company or its setting is static at one extreme or chaotic with random change at the other. It reminds him that direction cannot be imposed upon the future development of his company without considering the total environment and the impact upon all the related subsystems of change made or recurring in any one of them. The complexity of a company's environment begins to appear more manageable as its relationships to other organizations and individuals is sorted out. The system includes, for example, relations between the firm and

1. *Federal government agencies.*
    a. *Regulatory,* including specialized agencies like the Federal Communications Commission, the Interstate Commerce Commission and general agencies like the Federal Trade Commission and the Securities and Exchange Commission.

b. *Supportive,* like the Department of Commerce and the Export-Import bank.

c. *Taxing,* i.e., the Internal Revenue Service.

2. *State and local government agencies,* also regulatory, supportive, and taxing.

3. *Associations, foundations, and universities.*

4. *Money markets,* including holders of notes, bonds, preferred and common stock.

5. *Markets for output,* including customers, distributors, licensees, subsidiaries, joint ventures, foreign importers.

6. *Markets for material inputs,* including mines, ore deposits, forests or real estate, equipment, suppliers, licensors, wholesalers, and again subsidiaries and joint ventures.

7. *Markets for human services,* including directors, executives, managers, scientists and technicians, functional specialists, supervisors, workers, labor unions, and service firms (principally legal and accounting).

8. *Competitors.*[3]

This conceptual approach is difficult and challenging, but promises eventually to reduce to rational analysis what is now the practicing manager's intuitive and fragmentary vision of the moving forces that offer opportunity to his firm and take it away.

In the meantime, some related research has been addressed to understanding how businessmen who are not conceptually or theoretically equipped go about obtaining strategic information about environmental change and to how this process might be improved. Frank J. Aguilar, in *Scanning the Business Environment,*[4] has pioneered a line of investigation that has been followed up

---

[3]This list is adapted from Exhibit 5, p. 33 of an unpublished document entitled "Outline of a System of Concepts for Environmental Analysis and Corporate Planning," by John D. Glover.

[4]Frank J. Aguilar, *Scanning the Business Environment* (New York: The Macmillan Company, 1967).

in several doctoral theses. Working within the chemical industry, Aguilar examined first the ways in which executives looked for or obtained information about events and relationships in the environment outside the company, "the knowledge of which would assist top management in its task of charting the company's future course of action." He found few firms attempting any systematic means for gathering and evaluating strategic information.

The process of scanning the environment is viewed by Aguilar as having four modes, as follows:

1. "Undirected viewing"—the exposure to information without purpose, or knowledge of what issues might be raised.
2. "Conditioned viewing"—directed exposure, not involving active search, to an identified area or type of information but implying sensitivity to kinds of data and the readiness to assess their importance.
3. "Informal search"—limited and unstructured effort to get specific information for a specific purpose.
4. "Formal search"—deliberate effort following pre-established methodology to secure specific information relating to a specific issue.

These categories can be put together in a model which when animated may trace an inquiry from undirected to formal research or vice versa, with rules for choosing one mode of inquiry over another.

Examination of the practices of 41 companies in the United States and six European companies enables the author to classify the areas of external information obtained into five categories:

1. "Market Tidings," i.e., current activities in the market and the competitive field.
2. "Technical Tidings," i.e., technological developments.

3. Broad issues, i.e., events occurring outside the industrial environment.
4. Acquisition leads, i.e., suggestions for mergers, joint ventures, and acquisitions.
5. Other miscellaneous information.

Market tidings dominated the other categories and were of the most interest to all classes of managers.

The sources of this external information were, of course, outside and inside the company. External sources included personal sources predominantly, i.e., customers, suppliers, bankers, consultants, and other individuals from the circles in which executives moved. Impersonal outside sources were chiefly publications (which provided about 20 percent of the information acquired from all sources) but also included conferences, trade shows, exhibitions, and the like. Inside personal sources included peers, superiors, subordinates, and inside impersonal sources were comprised of regular and general reports and scheduled meetings. Surprisingly, superiors and in-company reports and meetings as sources of external information accounted for only 9 percent of the total.

The ways in which managers obtained information were classified according to whether it was solicited. If solicited, the information was further categorized as explicitly solicited or organizationally solicited. More information received in total was unsolicited than solicited. Again, very few people in subordinate positions felt they were getting useful strategic information from their superiors.

The obvious moral of this study for our present purposes—strongly supported by similar studies by Robert Collings in the investment services industries—is that the process of obtaining strategic information is far from being systematic, complete, or even really informative about anything except current developments. Such information as is received is gathered mostly through personal relationships and is thus screened only by the general reliability of the informant. These researches show that it is possible to organize better the gathering and integrating of environmental data through such means as bringing scanning activities together, assigning responsibility for them, coordinating information with planning, and communicating the information internally. The adequacy of a company's information-gathering capability and past performance can be appraised once the question is raised. The assessment of a company's informational needs can of course be completed only when its strategy is known or the strategic alternatives being considered have been identified. It will be done only if the need for information is understood in relation to the company's goals, policies, and plans.

At any rate, the complexity of a company's total environment, the rate at which change is taking place in whatever has been observed, and the incompleteness of conceptual apparatus for defining the relevant characteristics of the environment of a business do not constitute a good excuse for ignoring the problem. Some companies do indeed take steps to alert their organization generally to information oriented more to the future than is the current market activity, which apparently now comprises most of the information processed. The strategic implications of this information are usually implicit and easily missed. At a very simple level, the Xerox Corporation in 1967 asked 50 key executives and technical managers about what changes they expected by the year 2,000. A brief report was circulated in the company.[5] It is incomplete and of

---

[5]This report was published in *The Futurist,* April, 1969, pp. 35–36.

course as a forecast rather casual, but its impact must have stimulated those who thought about the questions and saw each other's answers. This same company, of course, makes use of systematic market research and very detailed projections of market growth in connection with its operating and long-range planning procedures.

The General Electric Company, through the Business Environment Section of its Corporate Personnel and Industrial Relations staff prepared in 1968 a more elaborate report entitled "Our Future Business Environment: Developing Trends and Institutions." A 65-page report and an eight-page summary of its findings were made available to the management of the company's divisions as requested. The findings are discussed in the company's executive education programs. The first report was updated a year later as a consequence of the comments received and of 1968–69 developments. The writers interviewed 60 authorities in universities, business and research associations, in press and government with a view of synthesizing predictions about the future and observations of the major forces reshaping American society. This study, which I draw from extensively in my illustrations of the kind of forces and trends that constitute the changing environment of business, was originally intended to suggest imaginative ideas and practical action to men who would be responsible for the company's human resources and its relations to its employees. It is much more widely applicable, but what actual use has been made has not yet been determined. Economic forecasts are fairly commonplace in industry but identification of social and political trends has been less so.

With a view probably toward stimulating a welcoming interest in innovation in its own company, the Kaiser Aluminum and Chemical Company through its unusual publication, *Kaiser Aluminum News,* frequently devotes issues not only to forces currently changing our environment, but to what lies ahead. Not so much a channel to new information as a stimulant to seeking it, the publication has attracted a great deal of attention to its content. Its impact upon the company cannot of course be separated from such other influences as its president's persistent interest in new opportunities and new ways to perform established tasks.

Opportunities to cooperate in developing ideas about the future are offered by such organizations as the Hudson Institute (Croton-on-Hudson, New York) and the Institute for the Future (Middletown, Connecticut). In 1969, Herman Kahn, author with Anthony J. Wiener of *The Year 2000: A Framework for Speculation* (New York: Macmillan Company, 1967) instituted a study entitled "The Future of the Corporation and the Environment for Management 1975–1985." The study will focus initially on three areas of corporate interest—"the impact of technological innovation, the impact of changing life styles and values, and the impact of the multi-national and international corporations." Thirty American and 30 foreign companies have been invited to participate in this study and to share the cost by contributing $12,000 each as a client. Reports of the study will be made available to the clients as it progresses, and personnel from client companies will work on the project. A larger continuing research project in "the future of the corporation and the environment for management" will also provide opportunity for the participation by interested companies.

The growth of organizations like the World Future Society and the National Society for Corporate Planning, to say nothing of new future-oriented courses in our universities, will provide stimulation, general knowledge, and possibly practical information to companies willing to become well-informed. Hard work, rather than occult powers, is what is required, for most of what will be important in the next 25 years is already visible or in motion. It remains only for that motion to be observed and its ultimate effect estimated. Successive corrections of estimates become possible so long as the development is not lost sight of. Once a company's management is convinced that nothing is so certain as change and that some changes are inevitable, it becomes free of the delusion that blinds executives to the opportunity to shape and influence the environment in which they are powerful participants. Given time and imagination, what cannot be shaped can be constructively adapted to.

It is clear that a systematic, dynamic, and reasonable updating of current expectations of what the future will be like will one day become a routine management activity. It is not now. As our whole society becomes more sensitive to the need for deliberate choice of national goals and for assigning resources and priorities for their achievement, the business firm will have available to it a wide range of support and research for its own predictions. As the art of looking ahead becomes more sophisticated and expectations of future development become established, the uncertainty attending forecasting will be reduced. One simple reason is that prophecies become self-fulfilling when they are widely subscribed to. An advanced society to a considerable extent can make happen what it decides either tacitly or explicitly should happen.

Identification of Opportunities and Risks

For the man who cannot know everything, and for the firm that has not embarked upon the systematic and continuous surveillance of environmental change, a few simple questions kept constantly in mind will serve to high-light changing opportunity and risk.

1. *What are the essential economic and technical characteristics of the industry in which the company participates?*

Whether these are in flux or not, they may define the restrictions and opportunities confronting the individual company and will certainly suggest strategy for it. For example, knowledge that the cement industry requires high investment in plant, proximity to a certain combination of raw materials, a relatively small labor force, and enormous fuel and transportation costs, suggests where to look for new plant sites and what will constitute competitive advantage and disadvantage. The nature of this product may suggest for a given company the wisdom of developing efficient pipeline and truck transportation and cheap energy sources rather than engaging in extensive research to achieve product differentiation or aggressive price competition to increase market share.

2. *What trends suggesting future change in economic and technical characteristics are apparent?*

Changes in demand for the product of one industry in competition with the products of another, and changes in the product itself, occurring as a result of research and development, affect the chance for growth. For example, the glass container industry's development of strong, light, disposable bottles recouped part of the market lost by glass to the metal container. The need for the glass industry to engage in this development effort was made apparent by the observable success of the metal beer can. Similarly, the easy-opening metal container suggested the need for an easily removable bottle cap. The physical characteristics of any product can be examined against the master trend toward simplicity, convenience, and serviceability in consumer goods and against competitive innovations.

3. *What is the nature of competition both within the industry and across industries?*

A small rubber company in an industry led by Uniroyal Inc., Goodyear, Goodrich, and Firestone, will not, under the economic condition of overcapacity, elect to provide the automobile business with original tires for new cars. The structure of competition, quite apart from the resources of the firm, may suggest that a relatively small firm should seek out a niche of relatively small attraction to the majors, and concentrate its powers on that limited segment of the market.

Present and developing competition usually extends, of course, beyond the industry in which a company finds itself. For example, the competition for the cement industry from producers of asphalt road-building materials is as important as that from other cement producers.

4. *What are the requirements for success in competition in the company's industry?*

In every industry some critical tasks must be performed particularly well to insure survival. In the ladies' belt and handbag business style and design are critical, but so (less obviously) are relationships with department store buyers. In the computer business, a sales force able to diagnose customer requirements for information systems, to design a suitable system, and to equip a customer to use it, is more important than the circuitry of the hardware.

Although the question of what tasks are most critical may be chiefly useful as a means of identifying risks or possible causes of failure, it may also suggest opportunity. Imagination in perceiving new requirements for success under changing conditions, when production-oriented competitors have not done so, can give a company a leadership position. For example, opportunity for a local radio station and the strategy it needed to follow, changed sharply with the rise of television, and those who first diagnosed the new requirements paid much less for stations than is now necessary.

5. *Given the technical, economic, social, and political developments that most directly apply, what is the range of strategy available to any company in this industry?*

The force of this question becomes obvious when we look, for example, at the drug industry. The speed and direction of pharmaceutical research, the structure of the industry, the characteristics of worldwide demand, the different and changing ideas about how adequate medical care should be made available to the world's population, the concern about price, and the nature of government regulation suggest some constraints within which a range of opportunity is still vividly clear. Similarly, in a more stable industry, there is always a choice. To determine its limits, an examination of environmental characteristics and developments is essential.

OPPORTUNITY AS A DETERMINANT OF STRATEGY

Awareness of the environment is necessarily a continuing requirement for informed choice of purposes, not a special project to be undertaken only when warning of change becomes deafening. Planned exploitation of changing opportunity usually follows an orderly course which both permits and provides increasing awareness of areas to which a company's capabilities may be profitably extended. For a typical company, which is governed by the determination that after a dividend adequate to maintain stockholder confidence profits will be reinvested, the search for opportunity appears to take a variety of forms.

First, within its domestic market, a company will try to increase its volume, to expand the market, and to increase its market share. This step does not require a changed strategy but a more intensive implementation. Policies regarding quality, service, price, promotion, and sales management will be shaped in detail to reflect extensive knowledge of a relatively specialized area of business. In response to detailed awareness of market need, the product will appear in a variety of forms and will proliferate into a family of related items, like a full range of small motors or a series of breakfast foods. The opportunity for growth stems from increase of demand, and competitive success is measured by increased market share.

If the original strategy proves workable in its original sphere, the growing company will typically move next into new geographical areas, either within a large domestic market like the United States or overseas. The product-market combinations remain the same. Macroeconomic and political developments have opened the world to companies not confined by law to their domestic markets. The American firm no longer limits its search for opportunity to the continental United States. The growth of free trade, the relative stability of East-West relations, the appearance of the management contract as an opportunity for free enterprise in socialist economies, and the development abroad of consumer purchasing power mean a marked geographical expansion of opportunity. The consequence is that the strategist's interests and information must henceforth be global in extent. Geographical expansion of the sphere of the original strategy thus introduces the problem of systematizing intelligence to which we have already alluded.

A growing company that has successfully extended its activities to wider geographic areas is thereafter likely to enlarge its operations and the scope of its strategy by reaching forward toward the ultimate consumer or backward to the sources of supply. Vertical integration is logically the next step, since the firm's knowledge of its environment will naturally focus its attention on opportunities in those areas that are most closely related to original activities. Furthermore, geographical expansion may well involve acquisitions and mergers of firms that are integrated in varying degrees. The growth of the oil industry is a classic example of both geographical expansion and vertical integration.

Once a company has successfully come to terms with its original milieu, has expanded its market geographically, and has extended the range of the related functions it performs in its markets, then it is likely to seek still further growth by diversifying its product line horizontally. Product diversification of this type imposes the most severe requirements, since it calls for knowledge of present situations and future possibilities in industries where the company has no prior experience to guide it.

Theoretically, then, the course of growth finally spans the full range of business activity for any firm not limited by special legislation. The identification of opportunity in the context of risk is simplest in the instance of the manufacturer of a single product sold within a clearly defined geographical area to meet a known demand. As geographical coverage is extended, or more stages are added in the making of a product, or the product becomes a line of related products via vertical integration, more attention to a more complex pattern of environmental forces is required. For example, the proprietor of a small engineering company specializing in electromechanical devices—unless he wishes to grow greatly—need not concern himself with anything besides meeting the demand for his highly specialized products and making sure that, whatever happens, enough demand remains to sustain his company. He need spend on the state of the world less time than the few minutes he devotes every hour to overseeing his entire production operation. The chairman of General Electric, on the other hand, would be hard put to it to identify any significant political, social, economic, or technological development in the world that did not have some influence on the future strategic opportunity of his company.

The multiplication of strategic alternatives which accompanies the progress of a single enterprise along the course just sketched presents, finally, problems which escape solution. The more one finds out what might be done, the harder it is to make the final choice. The demonstrated existence of an opportunity is not an adequate basis for the decision to seek it out. Before we pass to the other factors that must be considered, two consequences of the development pattern we have described should be clearly defined. They will be of great importance for a growing company in pondering its proper decision.

First, the sheer number of alternatives which will be disclosed by a well-directed scrutiny of world markets constitutes an embarrassment of riches. Some large firms, slow to make the decision to become multinational, seem now to have Klondike fever on a global scale. Those who refuse to go everywhere at once do not find choice easy. For example, McGraw-Hill has the good fortune to have an economic opportunity of enormous proportions for its future expansion. Its distinctive strategy of furnishing technical and scientific information to particular groups previously identified as having a special need for these data is obviously applicable to all countries of the world where education is transforming the life of the people and technical progress is nurturing a growing need for more information. The problem for McGraw-Hill is not where opportunity exists for expansion overseas—it is everywhere—but which opportunity to pursue first. This choice begins in the determination of potential return, and though it does not end there, the ranking of alternatives in order of their economic significance is probably the first step.

The objective assessment of opportunity is difficult because of the unreliability of statistical information in developing countries and the hazards of predicting the political, social, and technical developments in a given area. But with the assignment of sufficient analytical brainpower to the task, a degree of order can be imposed upon the range of alternatives available. The investment in this activity is preferable to opening up operations in all countries at once on the grounds that some will succeed, or to acquiring any business that foreign nationals decide to sell to Americans at what their local competitors consider an outrageous price.

The diversified company has another problem different from that of trying to make the best choice among many. If it has divisionalized its operations and strategies, as sooner or later in the course of diversification it must, then divisional opportunities come into competition with each other.

The corporate management will wish to invest profits not distributed to stockholders in those opportunities that will produce the greatest return to the corporation, and, if need be, management will be willing to let an individual division decline if its future looks less attractive than that of others. The division will wish to protect its own market position, ward off adverse developments, prolong its own existence, and provide for its own growth. The division manager, who is not rewarded for failures, will program projects of safe but usually not dramatic prospects. The claims regarding projected return on investment, which are submitted in all honesty as the divisional estimate of future opportunity, can be assumed to be biased by the division's regard for its own interest and the manager's awareness of measurement.

The corporate management cannot be expected to be able to make independent judgments about all the proposals for growth which are submitted by all the divisions. On the other hand, all divisions cannot be given their heads, if the corporation's needs for present profit are to be met and if funds for reinvestment are limited. In a decentralized organization, it is inappropriate to centralize planning. In any case, the greatest knowledge about the opportunities for a given technology and set of markets should be found at the divisional level.[6]

The resource allocation problem in a diversified company has not been well understood, either by practicing executives or students of capital budgeting. Far more than an economic process of ranking projects by magnitude of expected return, involving complex and controversial concepts of measurement, the allocation decision is embedded in political, organizational, and communication processes which often do not permit achieving a strategically correct outcome. Joseph L. Bower, whose *Managing the Resource Allocation Process: A Study of Corporate Planning and Investment*[7] is a ground-breaking study of investment processes from a general management point of view, finds that traditional financial techniques for

---

[6]See Norman Berg, "Strategic Planning in Conglomerate Companies," *Harvard Business Review,* May-June, 1965, pp. 79–92.

[7]Published by the Division of Research, Harvard Business School, Soldiers Field, Boston, Massachusetts 02163 in 1970.

investment projects typically separate projects from the business they are meant to serve, produce severe distortions in focus and timing, and disrupt the coordination of divisional activities with the optimal course for the corporation. He concludes that strategic planning and investment planning must as processes be closely interrelated. The evaluation of investment is affected by formal organization, salary and bonus plan administration, the accounting system, and the selection of executives for advancement.

This important study maps the route to an improved capital allocation process serving strategic ends and to the solution of a problem much more complex than it has been thought to be.

The strategic dilemma of a conglomerate world enterprise, however, is one that may not have a satisfactory solution. When the range of what must be known exceeds the capacity—as these days it soon does—of a single mind, and when the range of a company's activities spans many industries and technologies, the problems of formulating a coherent strategy get out of hand. If the identification of opportunity results in its being pursued without regard for any consideration other than return on investment, then total performance is likely, in the long run, to become at best mediocre.

We have said that the identification of opportunities and risks in the environment of a company committed to growth will lead it to increase its volume in a given market, to develop products related to its original product, to expand geographically, to integrate vertically, and ultimately to diversify its product line.

There is available to the corporate strategist another model of the stages of development through which a corporation passes. Bruce Scott[8] and Malcolm S. Salter, re-spectively, have in two unpublished theses and several working papers for their colleagues, outlined first a three and later a four-stage categorization of the outcomes of growth and success in adaptation to opportunity. Their fundamental hypothesis is that most businesses can be placed somewhere in a spectrum extending from very simple to very complex forms as, in response to market op-portunity, growth occurs in the number of products, cov-erage of markets, and overall size. Three points along this spectrum were designated by Scott as "stages" as follows:

Stage 1—proprietorships and small companies with no spe-cialized functions, as exemplified in small com-panies entirely managed by one man and supplying a single related line of products through a single channel of distribution to a single market.

Stage 2—a single unit company manufacturing a technologi-cally related line of products, larger in size and specialized in function (e.g., sales, finance, and production) managed by a group of executives.

Stage 3—a firm with multiple operating units in which geo-graphically decentralized units buy and sell in the marketplace and to each other through their own channels.

To this pattern Salter[9] adds a breakout of Scott's original Stage 3.

---

[8]Bruce R. Scott, *An Open System Model of the Firm* (unpublished doctoral dissertation deposited in Baker Library of the Harvard Business School, 1963).

[9]Malcolm S. Salter, "Stages of Corporate Development" (unpublished policy paper, Harvard Business School, 1968—a derivative of his thesis entitled *Stages of Corporate Development: Implications for Manage-ment Control*).

Stage 4—a multi-product, multi-market firm decentralized
in operations and management. Here external
market transactions between the divisions and their
markets dominate interdivisional transactions.

The importance of the early work in establishing a pattern of corporate development (more useful, for example,
than earlier attempts to make the corporation analogous
in organic development to an animal) is probably in relating organization structure to growth and to predicting the
evolution of patterns of management in a company as it
grows. It may define a natural course of evolution which
can be directed but could hardly be prevented. When we
come to consider the relationship of organizational structure and relationships, this model will prove informative.
In the meantime, we should note that the total development of a firm, including its organization structure, is dependent on the evolution of product-market relationships.

To return, then, to the crucial decisions about what
product line to address to what evolving market opportunity, we assume that the management of a company
wishes to retain control over its strategy, no matter how
inexorable is the pattern of its development. From the
point of view of maintaining control of strategy, the critical step is diversification away from the company's original business. Guided by a strategic concept of the nature
of the enterprise and the unity of its businesses, a company may successfully enter fields that appear to be different but are fundamentally related. Guided only by the
entrepreneurial estimate of attractive return on investment or by the opportunistic impulse to embark on a new
venture, the large diversified enterprise may find itself unable to compete effectively with more specialized firms
which are better able to know what they should do.

Though it may be equal to capitalizing on the present opportunity, it may not be able to solve the problem of resource allocation posed by future requirements.

To decide which is the best among several opportunities identified by informed examination is a task that requires more than economic analysis. If the difficulties inherent in following through on new undertakings in a swiftly changing world are to remain manageable, then some criterion for choice besides the opportunity for profit must be observed. Economic opportunity abounds, but not the ability to capture it. For example, a company jaded by shrinking margins may be tempted by the fortunes to be made in land development in Australia. The old Underwood Company, once the leading manufacturer of typewriters in the world, thought in the years before its acquisition by Olivetti that it should diversify into computers. But the fact that there is much money to be made in a new field or in a strong growth industry does not mean that a company with abilities developed in a different field is going to make it. We must turn now to the critical factors which for an individual company make one good opportunity better than another.

Determining Corporate Competence and Resources

The first step in validating a tentative choice among several opportunities is to determine whether the organization has the capacity to prosecute it successfully. The capability of an organization is its demonstrated and potential ability to accomplish, against the opposition of circumstance or competition, whatever it sets out to do. Every organization has actual and potential strengths and weaknesses. Since it is prudent in formulating strategy to extend or maximize the one and contain or minimize the other, it is important to try to determine what they are and to distinguish one from the other.

The simple but highly useful first observation must be that it is indeed just as possible for a company to know its own strengths and limitations as it is to maintain a workable surveillance of its changing environment. That the problems of subjectivity and a tendency to underestimate potential strength are as knotty as those of uncertainty in forecasting should not deter a company from trying to know itself.

Howard H. Stevenson has made the first formal study of management practice in defining corporate strengths and weaknesses as part of the strategic planning process.[10] He looked at five aspects of the process: the attributes of the company which its managers examined, the organizational scope of the strengths and weaknesses identified, the measurement employed in the process of definition, the criteria for telling a strength from a weakness, and the sources of relevant information. As might be expected, the process Stevenson was looking at was imperfectly and variously practiced in the half dozen companies he studied. He found that the problems of definition of corporate strengths and weaknesses, very different from those of other planning processes, center mostly on a general lack of agreement on suitable definition, criteria, and information. For an art that has hardly made a beginning, Stevenson offers a prescriptive model for integrating the considerations affecting definition of strength or weakness. It is indicative of the primitive stage of some of our concepts for general management, that Stevenson's most important conclusion is that, for now, the at-

---

[10]See Howard H. Stevenson, *Defining Corporate Strengths and Weaknesses: An Exploratory Study* (an unpublished doctoral thesis deposited in Baker Library, Harvard Business School, 1969).

tempt to define strengths and weaknesses is more useful than the usual final product of the process.

This usefulness can be partially illustrated from a company not included in Stevenson's study. In 1959, a new president took over the management of the dominant worldwide manufacturer of sewing machines, which in our case studies of this firm we call the International Manufacturing Company, though the disguise is quite transparent. His company was not producing, in his judgment, a proper return on the huge amounts of capital invested in the sewing machine business. Reduction of the assets employed was about to provide the company with obviously one great strength—substantial funds for investment in other businesses. The president addressed to the members of a committee he had established to develop a diversification strategy a memorandum on criteria for diversification. His second criterion, involving a conscious consideration of company strengths, is as follows:[11]

1. We are an operating company and not an investment company. We should therefore seek new businesses which we can manage rather than those in which we would be a mere investor contributing nothing but money. As a mere investor we would be at a disadvantage relative to those companies and firms which make a profession of investment.

2. The new fields should be compatible with our existing business and should fit the kind of company we are, or rather the kind of company we are in the process of becoming. This means that they should utilize broad areas of special assets, skills, and abilities which we have or are acquiring. It seems to me that this utilization of

---

[11]Quoted from "International Manufacturing Corporation (B1)," in Learned, Christensen, Andrews, and Guth, *Business Policy: Text and Cases* (Homewood, Illinois: Richard D. Irwin, Inc., 1965), pp. 957–59.

special capabilities is probably the most important factor in successful diversification. It reduces the risks of diversification and insures against becoming a mere holding company with a congeries of unrelated and disparate businesses. The following is a list, probably incomplete, of our special assets and capabilities.

a) Our name and reputation. While this asset is unique, its importance would vary considerably dependent on the type of new business being considered. Geographically, this asset is of greater importance abroad than in the United States.

b) Our ability and experience in operating abroad. This is perhaps our most distinctive asset. It is worldwide and extends through engineering, production, distribution, marketing, finance, and general management and comprises a body of talent and experience that has few, if any, counterparts.

c) Our engineering and production ability in the field of precision manufacture of high-quality mechanical products containing numerous small parts. Here one must be careful in definition. We have no particular talent for low-cost manufacture. Our abilities lie in the field of products where quality is relatively more important than low manufacturing cost.

d) Our engineering and production ability in the field of manufacture of high-quality wood products. Generally speaking, the same qualification applies here.

e) Our marketing ability in the field of sales to consumers of mechanical products requiring demonstration, instruction and service. Here again some qualification is necessary. Our distribution and selling methods are expensive and require large investment. We have no special abilities in fields requiring low-cost mass-distribution techniques, nor do we have, except here and there abroad, any particular talent and experience in using an uncontrolled distributing and selling organization.

f) Our marketing ability in the field of sales to industrial users of precision production equipment with a large service factor. I believe our abilities here are actually of wider potential for diversification than those associated with our family sales methods. The I.S.D. [Industrial Sales Department] marketing techniques are far less expensive and less specialized and are similar to those employed generally in marketing production equipment to industry.

g) Our experience in extending, collecting, and financing installment credit. There are many counterparts of this in the United States but few abroad, so this ability is relatively more unusual abroad.

h) Our greatly increased research and development capability as a result of the expansion of the Research Division and the acquisition of Research Operations. While presently these facilities are overtaxed, they provide a broad, sound base upon which a large expansion into new product development could be undertaken.

i) We have at Penbrook [Roscoe Motors, Inc.], Research Operations and Babylon a combination of research, engineering, and manufacturing abilities in the general field of electronic instruments and devices which, while difficult to define, is nevertheless already an important capability and will be more important in the future as the military program progresses. One of our long-range objectives in entering the military field was to participate in the technological progress which at the present time characterizes military work, with the expectation that techniques and products would be developed which would have civilian applications. It is already apparent that there are a number of areas that appear to be promising in this respect. This will not come about automatically, however, but will require the funding of projects to investigate the civilian application of products or techniques developed for the military. A project is currently being organized at

Research Operations and Penbrook to make a large test of the possibilities of going into the field of special purpose electronic data processing equipment. While the origin of this was some work started at Penbrook a couple of years ago, which we supported rather than the military, it nevertheless exemplifies how capabilities of this type can lead into civilian fields.

j) We have acquired in the last three years a substantial amount of experience in the pulp industry and some of our people have now been trained in this industry. While these capabilities have not been acquired without heavy expense, they nevertheless represent a growing fund of experience and talent in this new field.

3. A very important part of a diversification program would be to establish some minimum size for any new endeavor so as to avoid too great a dispersion of effort. A new business requires in its early years a wholly disproportionate amount of management time and talent and a small project requires practically as much of this important and limited ingredient as does a large one. A new field which does not have the potential of, say, one million dollars of pretax profit within the foreseeable future would probably be too small to bother with. Such a limitation, however, would not be applicable in the case of new products fitted into the product line of an existing segment of the organization but rather in the case of entry into a truly new business. However, even in the former case, it is well to have in mind the wisdom of not dispersing efforts over a large number of small projects no one of which is large enough to justify a major effort.

4. New businesses and new products should be analyzed primarily from the point of view of establishing the requirements for success in the new field rather than from a starting point that assumes that the new activity must be fitted into some existing International facilities or organization. Other things being equal, the employment of existing facilities or the provision of work for existing

employees would be important added advantages, but these cannot be primary considerations without unduly limiting the available opportunities or handicapping the new venture.

5. We should go into new businesses only if we are fully prepared to take on all of the functions and responsibilities commonly encountered in the new field. In many cases in the past we have tended to think primarily of manufacture and have not given adequate attention to marketing or research and development. In fact, we have endeavored to avoid taking on any marketing function and have not given proper weight to the importance of research. To my mind, success in a new field would be quite dependent upon an all-out effort comprising all the functional areas which are important in the new industry. In most cases I believe we shall find that the most critical area is marketing and the next most critical is research and development.

6. One of the most important requirements is that any new field should be one which has a large potential for growth. The sewing machine business is an old industry characterized by relatively high market saturation, low profit margins, intense price competition, and limited opportunity for basic technological progress. New and growing industries tend to have, in each respect, the opposite characteristics. In the United States I think it can almost be stated as a general rule that growth industries are those which are characterized by very high rates of technological progress. Abroad, the opportunities for growth appear to lie more in the direction of industries which will be able to supply the products demanded by the tremendous increase in the purchasing power of the middle classes of the population. This time is already upon us as far as Europe is concerned, as has been brought out in the studies made for us by the Stanford Research Institute. Even in the less well-developed countries this process is starting and will be very important for the

future. While it is difficult to generalize in this field, it may be important to direct our effort in the United States toward industries employing advanced technology while abroad consideration could be given to those fields which have had their period of large growth in America but are just entering this phase in Europe and will enter it later in less well-developed areas.

This president, other data make clear, had an equally definite but less publishable idea of what the weaknesses of his company were. These included its functional organization structure, the lack of delegated profit responsibility, the absence of effective control and accounting systems, an insensitivity to marketing opportunities, and obsolescence in the main product line. These he set out to remedy as consideration of new opportunities was guided by the general assent to his listing of the company's strengths.

The strengths of a company which constitute a resource for growth and diversification accrue primarily through experience in making and marketing a product line. They inhere as well in (1) the developing strengths and weaknesses of the individuals comprising the organization, (2) the degree to which individual capability is effectively applied to the common task, and (3) the quality of coordination of individual and group effort.

The experience gained through successful execution of a strategy centered upon one goal may unexpectedly develop capabilities which could be applied to different ends. Whether they should be so applied is another question. For example, a manufacturer of salt can strengthen his competitive position by offering his customers salt-dispensing equipment. If, in the course of making engineering improvements in this equipment, a new solenoid principle is perfected that has application to many industrial switching problems, should this patentable and marketable innovation be exploited? The answer would turn not only on whether economic analysis of the opportunity shows this to be a durable and profitable possibility, but also on whether the organization can muster the financial, manufacturing, and marketing strength to exploit the discovery. The former question is likely to have a more positive answer than the latter. In this connection, it seems important to remember that individual and unsupported flashes of strength are not as dependable as the gradually accumulated product- and market-related fruits of experience.

Even where competence to exploit an opportunity is nurtured by experience in related fields, the level of that competence may be too low for any great reliance to be placed upon it. Thus, a chain of children's clothing stores might well acquire the administrative, merchandising, buying, and selling skills that would permit it to add departments in women's wear. Similarly, a sales force effective in distributing typewriters may gain proficiency in selling office machinery and supplies. But even here it would be well to ask what distinctive ability these companies could bring to the retailing of soft goods or office equipment to attract customers away from competitors.

The "distinctive competence"[12] of an organization is more than what it can do; it is what it can do particularly well. Thus, the hapless manufacturer of chocolate candy who finally lost his chain of candy stores was not really a surpassingly efficient retailer of candy. He just thought he was. His real skill lay in production, in his ability to design special machinery to permit quality production at low cost. The proper application of his real strengths

---

[12]This phrase is used by Philip Selznick, *Leadership in Administration* (Evanston, Ill.: Row, Peterson & Co., 1957), p. 42.

would probably have confined him to manufacturing for wholesalers and supermarket chains.

To identify the less obvious or by-product strengths of an organization, which may well be transferable to some more profitable new opportunity, one might well begin by examining the organization's current product line and by defining the functions it serves in its markets. Almost any important consumer product has functions which are related to others into which a qualified company might move. The typewriter, for example, is more than the simple machine for mechanizing handwriting that it appears to be when looked at only from the point of view of its designer and manufacturer. If closely analyzed from the point of view of the potential user, the typewriter will be found to contribute to a broad range of information processing functions. Any one of these might suggest an area to be exploited by a typewriter manufacturer. Thus, the definition of product that would lead to identification of transferable skills must obviously be expressed in terms of the market needs it may fill rather than the engineering specifications to which it conforms.

Besides looking at the uses or functions to which his present product line contributes, the would-be diversifier might profitably identify the skills that underlie whatever success he has achieved. A watch manufacturer, for example, must have design and engineering skills, and he could apply these to other small precision products. It might be more likely, however, that success in this competitive industry turns less on design and engineering (obvious requirements, whose incidence is widespread) than on special skills in international marketing (a more subtle need, and a capability that seems relatively rare in the watch industry). Perhaps, then, merchandising skill could provide a basis for diversification by a successful manufacturer of watches. If so, it is again something quite different from the physical characteristics of a product that provides the clue a company should follow in seeking new areas for growth.

The insight required to perceive in the humdrum qualifications of an organization efficient at performing its long-accustomed tasks the essential strength to justify new ventures does not come naturally. Its cultivation can probably be helped by recognition of the need for analysis. In any case, we should look beyond the company's capacity to invent new products. Product leadership is not possible for a majority of companies, so it is fortunate that patentable new products are not the only major highway to new opportunities. Other avenues include new marketing services, new methods of distribution, new values in quality-price combinations, and creative merchandising. The effort to find or create a competence that is truly distinctive may hold the real key to a company's success or even to its future development. For example, the ability of our cement manufacturer (to spare our candy manufacturer this time) to run a truck fleet more effectively than his competitors may constitute one of his principal competitive strengths in selling an undifferentiated product. Similarly, the ability of Crown Cork and Seal to provide prompt delivery on specialty containers sets this company apart from its larger competitors whose forte is to provide standard cans at lower prices. Unless Crown's skill in giving fast service on nonstandard items proves limited to specialty containers, it might be extended to other products and activities—for instance, to fast service on equipment breakdowns. But even if the company never leaves the container industry, there are many additional markets overseas in which it can employ its inconspicuous but highly valuable abilities.

The way, then, to narrow the range of alternatives is to match opportunity to competence, once each has been accurately identified and its future significance estimated. It is this combination which establishes a company's economic mission and its relationship to its environment. The match is designed to minimize organizational weakness and to maximize strength. In any case, risk attends it. And when opportunity seems to outrun present distinctive competence, the willingness to gamble that the latter can be built up to the required level is almost indispensable to a strategy that challenges the organization and the people in it. It appears to be true, in any case, that the potential capability of a company tends to be underestimated. Organizations, like individuals, rise to occasions, particularly when the latter provide attractive reward for the effort required.

Before we leave the creative act of putting together a company's unique internal capability and evolving opportunity in the external world, we should note that—aside from distinctive competence—the principal resources found in any company are money and people—technical and managerial people. At this stage of economic development, money seems less a problem than technical competence, and the latter much less critical than managerial competence. We must look also at managerial capacity and, without underestimating it, we must not assume that it can rise to any occasion. The recent vigorous diversification of American industry is marked by hundreds of instances in which a company strong in one endeavor lacked the ability to manage an enterprise requiring different skills. The right to make handsome profits over a long time period must be earned. Opportunism without competence is a garden path. Where it leads cannot be predicted, but in any case it is beyond the confines of a sober essay in praise of predetermined purpose.

Besides equating an appraisal of market opportunity and organizational capability, the decision to make and market a particular product or service should be accompanied by an identification of the nature of the business and the kind of company management desires. Such a guiding concept is a product of many considerations, including the management's personal values. As such, this concept will change more slowly than other aspects of the organization, and it will give coherence to all the various company activities. For example, a president who is determined to make his firm into a worldwide producer and fabricator of a basic metal, through policies differentiating it from the industry leader, will not be distracted by excess capacity in developed markets, low metal prices, and cutthroat competition in certain markets. Such a firm should not be sidetracked into acquiring, for example, the Pepsi-Cola franchise in Africa, even if this business promised to yield a good profit. (That such a firm should have an experimental division exploring offshoot technology is, however, entirely appropriate.)

In each company, the way in which distinctive competence, organizational resources, and organizational values are combined is unique. Differences among companies are as numerous as differences among individuals. The combinations of opportunity to which distinctive competencies, resources, and values may be applied are equally extensive. Generalizing about how to make an effective match is less rewarding than working at it. The effort is a highly stimulating and challenging exercise. The outcome will be unique for each case and each situation.

The achievement of an economic strategy suitably matching opportunity, resources, and competence vastly simplifies the task of optimizing over time return to the shareholders and indeed the value of their investment.

The strategist who would design an economic set of objectives and policies for his business could profitably bring to the task not only the questions suggested earlier, but the following as well:

What really is our product line? What functions does it serve? To what additional functions might it be extended or adapted?

What is happening to the market for our products? Is it expanding or contracting? Why?

What are our company's major strengths and weaknesses? From what sources do these arise?

What is our strategy? Is the combination of product and market an optimum economic strategy? Is the central nature of our business clear enough to provide us with a criterion for product diversification?

What, if any, better combinations of market opportunities and distinctive competence can our company effect, within a range of reasonable risk?

These questions will prove helpful throughout the task of designing an economic strategy. However, they are never wholly sufficient, for the strategic decision is never wholly economic in character.

The Company and Its Strategists: Relating Economic Strategy and Personal Values

UP TO THIS POINT we have argued that a concept of purpose and a sense of direction strengthen a company's ability to survive in changing circumstances. We have seen, to be sure, the difficulties of understanding clearly both a company's circumstances and its strengths and weaknesses. The action implied by these difficulties has been an objective and well-informed surveillance of environment for threats and opportunities and a detached appraisal of organizational characteristics in order to identify distinctive competence. We have considered the suitable combination of a company's strengths and its opportunities to be a logical exercise characterized by perhaps not precise but reasoned, well-informed choices of alternatives assuring the highest possible profit. We have been examining the changing relationship of company and environment as if a purely economic strategy, uncontaminated by the personality or goals of the decision maker, were possible.

STRATEGY AS PROJECTION OF PREFERENCE

We must acknowledge at this point that there is no way to divorce the decision that names the most sensible economic strategy for a company from the personal values of those who make the choice. Executives in charge of company destinies do not look exclusively at what a company might do and can do. In apparent disregard of the second of these considerations, they sometimes seem heavily influenced by what they personally *want* to do.

We are ourselves not aware of how much desire affects our own choice of alternatives, but we can see it in others. Note, for example, George Romney's dramatic promotion of economic sensible transportation and the small car in the early days of American Motors and his subsequent repayment of all debt, in place of investment through research in the development of variations in the small car which might have retained leadership in an important segment of the market. Almost certainly we see reflected here the higher value Romney placed on economy than on consumer preferences, on liquidity over debt, and other values derived more from his character and upbringing than from an objective monitoring of the best course for American Motors to follow.[1] Frank Farwell

---

[1]See "American Motors Corporation (A) and (D)" in Learned, Christensen, Andrews, and Guth, *Business Policy: Text and Cases,* revised edition, 1969, pp. 60–117.

came from IBM to the presidency of Underwood in 1955, it has been said, saying that he would be damned if he would spend his life peddling adding machines and typewriters.[2] This aversion may explain why Underwood plunged into the computer business without the technical, financial, or marketing resources necessary to succeed in it. Similarly, when Adriano Olivetti purchased control of Underwood after three days of hurried negotiations, he may well have been moved by his childhood memory of visiting Hartford and by the respect for once the world's leading manufacturer of typewriters that led his father to erect in Ivrea a replica of the red-brick five-story Hartford plant.[3] That he wanted to purchase Underwood so badly may explain why he and his associates did not find out how dangerously it had decayed and how near bankruptcy it had been brought. The three presidents of J. I. Case in the years 1953 to 1963 seem to have been displaying their own temperaments as they wracked the company with alternatives of expansionism and contraction far beyond the needs of response to a cyclical industry environment.[4] In all these cases, the actions taken can be rationalized so as not to seem quite so personal as I have suggested they are.

We will be able to understand the strategic decision better if we admit rather than resist the dimension of preference. The professional manager in a large company, drilled in analytical technique and the use of staff trained to subordinate value-laden assumptions to tables of numbers, may often prefer the optimal economic strategy because of its very suitability. Certain entrepreneurs, whose

---

[2]See "Underwood-Olivetti (AR)," Learned, Christensen, Andrews, and Guth, *op. cit.* original edition, 1965, p. 229.

[3]*Ibid,* p. 33 ff.

[4]"J. I. Case Company," *ibid.,* pp. 82–102.

energy and personal drives far outweigh their formal
training and self-awareness, set their course in directions
not necessarily supported by logical appraisal. Such dis-
parity appears most frequently in small privately held
concerns, or in companies built by successful and self-
confident owner-managers. The phenomenon we are
discussing, however, may appear in any company.

Our problem now can be very simply stated. In examining the alternatives available to a company, we must
henceforth take into consideration the preferences of the
chief executive. Furthermore, we must also be concerned
with the values of other key managers who must either
contribute to or assent to the strategy if it is to be effective. We therefore have two kinds of reconciliation to
consider—first, the divergence between the chief executive's preference and the strategic choice which seems
most defensible and, second, the conflict among several
sets of managerial personal values which must be reconciled not only with an economic strategy but with each
other.

Thus, when Mr. Edgar Villchur, inventor of the acoustic suspension loudspeaker, founded Acoustic Research,
Inc.[5] in 1954, he institutionalized a desire to bring high
fidelity sound to the mass market at the lowest possible
cost. He licensed his competitors freely and finally gave
up his original patent rights altogether. He kept not only
his prices but his dealer margins low, maintained for considerable time a primitive production facility and an organization of friends rather than managers, and went to
great lengths to make the company a good place to work,
sharing with employees the company's success. The company was dominated by Mr. Villchur's desire to have a

---

[5]"Acoustic Research, Inc.," *ibid.,* pp. 327–484.

small organization characterized by academic, scientific, and intellectual rather than "commercial" values. Product development was led by some of these values away from the acoustical technology which Mr. Villchur's personal competence would have suggested into development of record players, amplifiers, and tuners which were to offer less in superiority over competitive products than did his speakers. Again, these were priced far below what might have been possible.

Mr. Abraham Hoffman, for years vice president and treasurer, had the task of trying to overcome his superior's reluctance to advertise, to admit the validity of the marketing function, and of maintaining the business as a profitable enterprise. That the company has succeeded in at long last developing and producing a music system of great value in relation to its cost and in winning the respect of the high fidelity listener market does not alter the fact that the first determination of strategy came more from Mr. Villchur's antibusiness values than from an analytical balancing of opportunity and distinctive competence. The latter would have led, with perhaps much greater growth and profitability, into acoustical systems, public address equipment, long-distance communications, hearing aids, noise suppression, and the like—all areas in which technical improvement in the quality of available sound are much needed.

We must remember, however, that it is out of Mr. Villchur's determination and goals that his company came into being in the first place. The extraordinary accomplishments of an antimarketing company in the marketplace are directly traceable to the determination to innovate in quality and price. The reconciliation between Mr. Villchur's values and Mr. Hoffman's more business-oriented determination to manage the company's growth more objectively occurred only when the company was sold to Teledyne, Mr. Villchur retired to his laboratory, and Mr. Hoffman became president. The quality achievements of this firm have been rewarded, but the economic potential of its strategy was for years unrealized.

We should in all realism admit that the personal desires, aspirations, and needs of the senior managers of a company actually *do* play an influential role in the determination of strategy. Against those who are offended by this idea either for its departure from the stereotype of single-minded economic man or for its implicit violation of responsibilities to the shareholder, I would argue that we must accept not only the inevitability but the desirability of this intervention. If we begin by saying that all strategic decisions must fall within the very broad limits of the manager's fiduciary responsibility to the owners of the business and perhaps to others in the management group,[6] then we may proceed legitimately to the idea that what a manager wants to do is not out of order. The conflict which often arises between what general managers want to do and what the dictates of economic strategy suggest they ought to do is best not denied or condemned. It should be accepted as a matter of course. In the study of organization behavior, we have long since concluded that the personal needs of the hourly worker must be taken seriously and at least partially satisfied as a means of securing the productive effort for which wages are paid. It should, then, come as no surprise to us that the president of the corporation also arrives at his work with his own needs and values, to say nothing of his relatively greater power to see that they are taken into account.

If we accept the inevitability of personal values in the

---

[6]See pp. 118 ff., "The Company and its Social Responsibilities: Relating Corporate Strategy and Public Expectations."

strategic decision that determines the character and the course of a corporation, then we must turn to the skills required to reconcile the optimal economic strategy with the personal preferences of the executives of the company. There is no reason why a better balance could not have been struck in Acoustic Research, without sacrifice to the genius of the founder or the quality of life in his company. It is first necessary to penetrate conventional rationalization and reticence to determine what these preferences are. For without this revelation, strategic proposals stemming from different unstated values come into conflict. This conflict cannot be reconciled by talking in terms of environmental data and corporate resources. The hidden agenda of corporate policy debates makes them endless and explains why so many companies do not have explicit, forthright, and usefully focused strategies.

In Acoustic Research, the needs of a growing business forced out the ex-music and dancing teachers who once worked for Mr. Villchur and led to successors with more management experience, but by now the company is strategically locked into its music systems rather than acoustical systems.

An opportunity for a more direct approach at an earlier stage to the reconciliation of divergence between personal preferences and corporate good sense can be found in Research, Inc.,[7] a small technical company founded in 1957 by three ex-professors and scientists. By 1958 the company had reached a strategic crossroads from which continued government-contract research and development, commercial exploitation of products derived from this research, and various combinations appeared possible. A goal of $10 million in sales within the following few years

---

[7]"Research, Inc.," Learned, Christensen, Andrews, and Guth, *op. cit.*, original edition, pp. 393–405. All names have been disguised.

raised the question of where to seek this growth—in contract research or commercial products. The firm had sold an important block of its stock to outside investors interested in growth and profit. The three founders of the company had left a technical research firm because of their aversion to what they called "the bureaucracy of a large organization." The chief scientist of the company, Dr. Wharfedale, was not really interested in growth at all; he wished to work on the design of projects so that interdisciplinary technical teams could go to work on them. He was opposed to commercial activity. Dr. Garrard, the president and technical director, expected to find the $10 million in sales in cost-plus-fixed-fee research contracts. He was confident that growth in government-sponsored research would continue and apparently that his company's profits (which he did not mention) would be adequate. Dr. Scott, the executive vice president and treasurer, was aware that the $10 million sales goal was a vague dream, concerned about the business aspects of the company's activities, and receptive to the idea that commercial products, in addition to the established operations research capability, would have to be developed. Mr. Marcello, vice president for administration, was brought into the company to encourage its growth. Alone of the top management, like Hoffman in Acoustic Research, he was concerned with profit and believed that expected return should be the principal criterion in developing the company's strategy.

The four top managers of this company, to oversimplify somewhat, are (in the values they brought to this problem) arranged in order from a scientific orientation (with academic values of freedom of inquiry and knowledge for its own sake, and smallness and informality of organization in dominant position) to a business orientation (with production efficiency, growth, and profitability high in the hierarchy of purpose). With Dr. Wharfedale at one extreme and Mr. Marcello at the other, with Garrard nearer Wharfedale, and Scott nearer Marcello, these differences in point of view assured difficulty in resolving strategy.

The actual outcome of this company's deliberations is too long a story to tell. In 1958 the possibilities for reconciliation seemed favorable. Each of the principals had no animosity for the others and at least some awareness of his own preferences. No one was so committed to academic values that he was about to return to a university and no one was so committed to business values that he wanted to discontinue Dr. Wharfedale's activities or to dispel the research atmosphere from his laboratories. It was Marcello's opportunity to lay before the others an analysis as of 1958 of the future amount and profitability of government work and to assess the prospects of the company's current and neglected commercial business. The company's capability was what it called operations research; it had no mass production capability whatever. The division of the company into two enterprises—one for contract research and one for commercial production (beginning with the present activities and gradually developing capability), with capital assigned to each in relation to its performance and prospects—would permit greater attention to profitability as a necessary result of continued growth. Production was segregated to separate sites and subsidiaries and an informal project arrangement was attempted in the research organization to keep small interdisciplinary groups in touch with each other and accustomed to forming and reforming around successive projects.

It would be easy to predict continuous tension between the two sides of the business and to expect more profit from one than from the other. But nothing appears beyond workable solution here, so long as the problem is addressed, the differences of point of view are made known, and a decision taken as to how the investment in growth is to be proportioned and results measured. The easy, but destructive outcome is to avoid conflict, to compromise interminably the definition of the company's dual businesses, to drift from decision to decision, yielding now to one set of values, later in recompense to another. Imagination, ingenuity, good will, and determination, all conspicuous in this company, should be able to build successive strategies balancing the economic and noneconomic rewards available to the company and its members. If the problem is not identified, however, it cannot be solved, in Research, Inc. or elsewhere.

To many caught up in the unresolved strategic questions in their own organizations, it seems futile even to attempt to reconcile a strategic alternative dictated by personal preference with other alternatives oriented toward capitalizing on opportunity to the greatest possible extent. In actuality, however, this additional complication poses fewer difficulties than at first appear. The analysis of opportunity and the appraisal of resources themselves often lead in different directions. To compose three, rather than two, divergent sets of considerations into a single pattern may increase the complexity of the task, but the integrating process is still the same. We can look for the dominant consideration and treat the others as constraints; we can probe the elements in conflict for the possibilities of reinterpretation or adjustment. We are not building a wall of irregular stone so much as balancing a mobile of elements, the motion of which is adjustable to the motion of the entire mobile.

As we have seen, external developments can be affected by company action and company resources, and internal competence can be developed. If worst comes to worst, it is better for a man to detach himself from a management whose values he does not share than to pretend he shares them or to wonder why they think as they do. Howard Head, whose passionate dedication to the metal ski not only produced a most successful business, but delayed unnecessarily its entry into plastic skis, has realistically retired from his now diversified business and has sold his holdings. It is not necessary, however, for all members of a management to think alike or to have the same personal values, so long as strategic decision is not delayed or rendered ineffective by these known and accepted differences. Large gains are possible simply by raising the strategic issues for discussion by top management, and by admitting the legitimacy of different preferences, and by explaining how superficial or fundamental the differences are.

Modification of Values

The question whether values can actually be changed during the reconciliation process is somewhat less clear. A value, for our purposes, is a "conception, explicit and implicit, distinctive of an individual or characteristic of a group, of the *desirable* which influences the selection of available modes, means, and ends of action."[8] Guth and Tagiuri emphasize that values are *concepts* of the desirable, not the "things, conditions, or ideas judged desirable as a result of applying the values to specific situations." Acquired early in life as the result of the "interplay of what he learned from those who reared him, and of his

---

[8]William D. Guth and Renato Tagiuri, "Personal Values and Corporate Strategy," *Harvard Business Review,* September-October, 1965, pp. 123–32. Quoted from Florence R. Kluckhohn *et al., Variations in Value Orientation* (Evanston, Ill.: Row, Peterson and Company, 1961).

particular individuality and 'times,' "[9] a person's basic values are a relatively stable feature of his personality, although they may change somewhat with his level of knowledge and analytical skill.

Nonetheless, the preference attached to ends in concrete circumstances is not beyond influence. The physicist in Research, Inc., who in his reflection of the values of pure science is opposed to commercial production, might withdraw his objection if he sees that his freedom to pursue his own projects can be better sustained by profits from operations than from government research contracts. Furthermore, his departure from the university and his present membership in the firm reflect some economic values and latent interest in profit for its own sake. He will retain the value orientation of the scientist, but may assent in this instance to the strategic alternative conceived in the value orientation of the businessman. At any rate, to presuppose that he would not do so is a common but futile approach to the value problem.

Guth and Tagiuri report some very interesting research which indicates that we may, in our use of stereotypes, ascribe much stronger value commitments to others than is justified. They report the results of a questionnaire regarding six basically different value orientations[10] that

---

[9]Guth and Tagiuri, *op. cit.*, p. 4.

[10]These are the six types identified by Edward Spranger, who classified all individuals as falling into one or another of the following:
1. *The Theoretical* (dominant intellectual interest in an empirical, critical, rational approach to systematic knowledge).
2. *The Economic* (orientation toward practical affairs, the production and consumption of goods, the uses and creation of wealth).
3. *The Aesthetic* (chief interest in the artistic, in form, symmetry, harmony, in experience for its own sake).
4. *The Social* (primary value the love of people and warmth of human relationships).
5. *The Political* (orientation toward power, influence, and recognition).
6. *The Religious* (mystical orientation toward unity and the creation of satisfying and meaningful relationship to the universe).

was administered to 178 R.&D. executives, 157 scientists, and 653 managers. Despite differences among these groups that might be assumed to exist, all three showed relatively high theoretical, economic, and political value orientations, and relatively low aesthetic, religious, and social values. Indeed, all three groups put theoretical values first.

A second finding of this study indicates that R.&D. executives see the scientist and the manager as exhibiting greater value differences than is actually the case. Thus, the scientist is viewed as much more dominantly theoretical than he actually is, the manager as much more dominantly economic and political. The latter's theoretical and religious orientation is seriously underestimated.

From these findings, two implications follow that merit particular emphasis at this point. First, the manager is much more "theoretically" oriented than the stereotype of the American businessman would indicate (but not, we would assert, more than his duties require). Second, values for these different groups may be easier to reconcile with each other and with requirements for a sound economic strategy than might at first be anticipated. Although one value orientation may be dominant in an individual and color his judgment of where opportunity lies and of what his company has power to achieve, other values are present, and effective appeal can be made to these by persons who want to influence the course of strategy. Sometimes, also, an appeal can be successful if it can show that a chosen strategy threatens the value it was designed to serve.

Thus, if the strikingly low price of the Acoustic Research turntable were to convey to the potential customers seeking highest quality that it was a second-rate or cheap product, the original purpose of the low price would be frustrated. If this could be shown, Mr. Villchur would doubtless consent to raise the price, solving meanwhile some other problems as well.

AWARENESS OF VALUES

Our interest in the role of personal values in strategic formulations should not be confined to assessing the influence of other people's values. Despite the well-known problems of introspection, we can probably do more to understand the relation of our own values to our choice of purpose than we can to change the values of others. Awareness that our own preference for an alternative opposed by another stems from values as much as from rational estimates of economic opportunity may have important consequences. First, it may make us more tolerant and less indignant when we perceive this relationship between recommendations and values in the formulations of others. Second, it will force us to consider how important it really is to us to maintain a particular value in making a particular decision. Third, it may give us insight to identify our bias and thus pave the way for a more objective assessment of all the strategic alternatives that are available. These consequences of self-examination will not end conflict, but they will at least prevent its unnecessary prolongation.

The object of this self-examination is not necessarily to endow us with the ability to persuade others to accept the strategic recommendations we consider best: it is to acquire insight into the problems of determining purpose and skill in the process of resolving them. The individual inquiring into his own values for the purpose of understanding his own position in policy debates can continue to assess his own personal opportunities, strengths and weaknesses, and basic values by means of the procedures outlined here. For a personal strategy, analytically considered and consciously developed, may be as useful to an individual as a corporate strategy is to a business institution. The effort, conducted by each individual, to formulate his personal purpose might well accompany his contributions to organizational purpose. If the encounter leads to a clarification of the purposes one seeks, the values one holds, and the alternatives available, the attempt to make personal use of the concept of strategy will prove extremely worthwhile.

Introducing personal preference forces us to deal with the possibility that the strategic decision we prefer (identified after the most nearly objective analysis of opportunity and resources we are capable of) is not acceptable to other executives with different values. Their acceptance of the strategy is necessary to its successful implementation. In diagnosing this conflict, we try to identify the values implicit in our own choice. As we look at the gap between the strategy which follows from our own values and that which would be appropriate to the values of our associates, we look to see whether the difference is fundamental or superficial. Then we look to see how the strategy we believe best matches opportunity and resources can be adapted to accommodate the values of those who will implement it. Reconciliation of the three principal determinants of strategy which we have so far considered is often possible by adjustment of any or all of the determinants.

We must not warp our strategy to the detriment of the company's future in order to adjust it to personal values. On the other hand, we should not expect to be able to impose an unwelcome pattern of purposes and policies on the people running a corporation. Strategy is a human construction; it must be responsive to human needs. It must ultimately inspire commitment. It must stir an organization to successful striving against competition. Somebody has to have his heart in it.

The Company and Its Social Responsibilities: Relating Corporate Strategy to the Needs of Society

WE HAVE COME at last to the fourth and final component of strategy—the moral and social implications of what was once considered a purely economic choice. In our consideration of strategic alternatives, we have so far moved from what the strategist *might* and *can* do to what he *wants* to do. We now move to what he *ought* to do—from the point of view of disinterested observers in society and his own standards of right and wrong. As we consider in this chapter the recommendation that strategic choice should meet ever rising moral and ethical stan-

118

dards, we will face at once the arguments of economic isolationists who retain from the past the conviction that business serves society best if it concentrates *solely* upon its economic function. We will examine also the newer, if sometimes ingenuous arguments of social interventionists who maintain that the management of business should and can concern itself with the problems of its physical and social environment.

We will see that the considerable consequences of accepting a doctrine of social responsibility for private business will require us to look for ways to reconcile the conflict in responsibility which occurs when profit and social contribution appear on the same corporate agenda. The creativity required to effect this reconciliation, that is, to make a company competitively successful by way of a corporate strategy that meets demands for responsibility from its members, its owners, and its customers, may well appear to us at last as the essence of the professionalization which is presently contributing both competence and conscience to the practice of management.

For professional managers who would submit their organizations to the discipline of an evolving strategy, coming to terms with the morality of choice is the most stimulating and strenuous problem in strategic decision-making. In the early 1970s it appears that the power of purpose in making individual and corporate life worthwhile will henceforth turn on its economic, esthetic, and moral quality. The economic quality of a corporate strategy can be quantitatively measured, though less certainly and much later than we sometimes think. Its humane and ethical qualities can be experienced and appraised less objectively but just as reliably by an educated and enlightened judgment, which need not falter for lack of relevant numbers. That this judgment will vary according to the values upon which it is based and within which it is exercised should not diminish its crucial importance. By now we should be reconciled to the differences in strategic decision which different values will produce, to the consequent healthy pluralism of an open industrial society, and to the strengths and weaknesses of democratic processes subjecting the behavior of all institutions to searching criticism.

THE CASE AGAINST VOLUNTARY ASSUMPTION OF SOCIAL RESPONSIBILITY

Although their influence is probably decreasing, many corporate executives and academic critics resist the tendency growing once tentatively and now massively through the last 50 years to invest management decision with social responsibility. By "social responsibility" we mean the intelligent and objective concern for the welfare of society that restrains individual and corporate behavior from ultimately destructive activities, no matter how immediately profitable, and leads in the direction of positive contributions to human betterment, variously as the latter may be defined. Proponents of the view that a firm's sole obligation is to maximize its profits agree generally that business should live up to its legal obligations: obey the Antitrust acts, keep honest expense accounts, label and weight out its product accurately, and pay its bills and taxes. The undesirable social consequences of business activity are left to the government to regulate or correct. The basis of the argument that profit seeking knows no other bounds is ultimately Adam Smith's *Wealth of Nations*. Classical economic theory postulates that in atomized markets, perfect competition produces not only the optimum allocation of economic resources but also satisfaction of the general interest. The "invisible hand" of competition keeps the self-seeking of men striving against each other from harming the public. In open markets serving consumers who are supposed to have complete knowledge of sources of supply and prices and to be motivated to make only the most economical purchases, the general good can best be served by the self-centered drive for survival and efficiency of the entrepreneur or small firm. The open market is conceptually what A. A. Berle has called an ethical balance wheel which levels out inequalities, eliminates the inefficient, and through competition prevents an undue concentration of power.

But the corporations, never expected by Adam Smith to amount to very much, have instead acquired substantial power. They have become in some cases virtually permanent institutions. Their power somewhat stabilizes price competition. They have secured customers who do not have perfect knowledge of alternatives and are not always persuaded to recognize the best one by its low price. We have come to a mixed economy, with imperfect competition, with various industries operating under varying degrees of public regulation and control, and with corporations sufficiently powerful to shape to an important extent their markets and environment.

Although the laissez-faire doctrine has long since been supplanted by more sophisticated economic practice and theory, its vestigial moral heritage is the recommendation that a businessman will best serve society by relentlessly pursuing efficiency and profit. Thus, Professor Reavis Cox of the Wharton School in *The Wall Street Journal* of October 15, 1969, while acknowledging the limitations of the invisible hand, asserts that the historic role of the businessman has been to "keep operating effectively the intricate mechanism by which man's material needs are met."

This is still all society should expect of him. Similarly, Andrew Hacker in *The New York Times Magazine* of November 17, 1963, decries as he always does, corporate involvement in social issues in similar terms. "The only responsibility of corporations is to make profits, thus contributing to a prosperous economic system."

Such observers often think highly of the economic function and consider it quite enough for the manager to worry about. It is the government's role, they usually believe, to check abuse, prescribe rules, codify the aspirations of the general public, and lead the way to solution of our society's problems. The belief that legislators and elected officials should remedy the social consequences of aggressive industrial activity is often accompanied by distrust of both the motives and capabilities of businessmen who seem willing to enter the arenas of public interest or assume responsibility for the social consequences of economic activity. Thus, Theodore Levitt, like Reavis Cox a professor of marketing, has said that the "Gospel of Social Responsibility," now so often deferred to in public speeches, is essentially hypocrisy. He believes that the need to show present profit is in business so great that self-interest *necessarily* excludes public service.[1] Hypocrisy, it may be said parenthetically, is worse to some sensibilities than the piracy it is presumed to mask. In the eye of candor, it is better for a businessman to be a forthright rather than a pious rascal. On the other hand, hypocrisy, which is said to be the homage vice pays to virtue, at least tells us which way the path of virtue is supposed to lead.

Naiveté, more the consequence of well-meaning incom-

---

[1]From a hitherto unpublished lecture at the Harvard Business School delivered on April 7, 1970. Similar views have been expressed by Levitt in "The Dangers of Social Responsibility," *Harvard Business Review,* September-October, 1958, pp. 41–50.

petence than a desire to deceive, is an additional charge brought by the conservative critics of business to attempts at responsibility. The innocence and the sudden disillusion with which some corporations have plunged into training unemployables, rebuilding ghettos, hiring members of disadvantaged minorities, and developing products and services for education, lend some credence to the argument that a businessman plays the fool outside his own sphere of making goods or contriving services and selling them for maximum gain. Inexperience, however, is not usually considered justification for inaction. It constitutes one persistent problem we know how to solve.

The conceptual leader of Cox, Levitt, and Hacker is Milton Friedman, whose *Capitalism and Freedom* argues that the doctrine of social responsibility is a "fundamentally subversive doctrine" in a free society. In such a society, "there is one and only one social responsibility of business—to use its resources and engage in activities designed to increase its profits so long as it stays within the rules of the game, which is to say, engages in open and free competition without deception or fraud."[2] His most recent statement equating social responsibility with socialism states again that the manager is the agent of the corporation's owners; his primary responsibility is to them. The desires of the stockholders are assumed to be making as much money as possible while conforming to the basic rules of the society. The manager who makes decisions affecting immediate profit by reducing pollution, for example, more than present law requires is in effect imposing taxes and acting without authority as a public employee.

---

[2]Milton Friedman, *Capitalism and Freedom* (Chicago, Illinois: The University of Chicago Press, 1962), p. 133. See also "The Social Responsibility of Business is to Increase its Profits," *New York Times Magazine*, September 13, 1970, pp. 32–33, 122–24, 126.

Friedman's argument assumes that the stockholder is Economic Man, interested only in maximum short-run profit with minimum deference to legal and ethical restraints. The courts, in upholding against stockholder suits the legality of corporate contribution to education, have suggested that stockholders themselves have responsibilities as citizens. The legality of corporate contributions to the public welfare implies that the managers of corporations are entitled to use their judgment in reconciling immediate return with future growth, maximum present profit with future return, corporate interests with the interests of the community. In actual practice, the stockholders of large publicly held corporations do not in the usual case pick directors, hire managers, or set the dividend rates. Except in recourse to their legal powers in case of emergency or rebellion, stockholders and institutional investors vote shares as management suggests. The actual power of an individual stockholder to give effect to his preference for maximum short-run profit is exercised not by changing management policy but by selling his stock.

In any case, the notion that the shareholder of a large, publicly held corporation is its owner grows increasingly indefensible. He owns shares, which represent so small a commitment on his part that he may through the mechanisms of the stockmarket shed it instantly. Management, to whom has come a virtually permanent delegation of authority for continuing direction of the publicly held corporation, is still bound to run the company to serve shareholder interest. But neither by law nor by custom does it have the simple obligation to pursue maximum profit.[3]

---

[3]This general thesis is developed in a brilliant article by J. A. C. Hetherington, "Fact and Legal Theory: Shareholders, Managers, and Corporate Social Responsibility," in the *Stanford Law Review*, January, 1969, pp. 248–92.

The complexity of present-day corporate practice means simply that the doctrine of maximum profit for the shareholders is most difficult to apply. The rules of the game, not always codifiable into law, are constantly changing. The manager of a publicly held corporation is increasingly seen as a professional person who must exercise independent judgment in deciding what combination of dividends and stock price will keep stockholders and maintain supply of capital and what combination of profit making and contribution to community well-being will best preserve future opportunity for his company and the business system of which it is a part. His strategy for satisfying the conflicting responsibilities besetting him will cause some stockholders to remain loyal and others to sell out. The investor has his own purposes, after all. In evaluating the behavior of the management of a firm, he may conclude that a company consciously considering issues of public interest which the law has not yet thrust upon it may ultimately be more profitable than one which tends only its short-run economic interests. There is no reason to suppose that over time a socially responsible management will make less money, pay fewer dividends, and achieve less appreciation of share price than the firm run by managers who are only as "responsible" as the law requires. Since the single-minded profit maximizer is likely to be so shortsighted that he misjudges changing market opportunity and the needs of his own organization, the shareholder as economic man needs both clairvoyance and the agility to sell in a hurry.

Beneath the argument that the corporate strategist should confine himself to his economic function and as neither hypocrite nor incompetent nor as anything else concern himself corporately with social problems is often a quite astringent view of the typical general manager's personal values, social concern, and capability. Ranging from skepticism to contempt, this estimate of business leadership is accompanied by the undocumented assumption that expertness in the social problems partially caused by industry lies outside industry in the universities or legislatures of the country. Apparently we are expected to believe that in educational institutions and legislative assemblies motives are more pure and knowledge of good and evil more advanced than in the world of affairs. Even nearer the root of the argument for isolationism is the undeniable central conflict in responsibility between the need on the one hand to make and show continually impressive profits in order to sustain price/earnings ratios and the market values of stockholders' equity, and the costs, on the other hand, of dealing with such byproducts of economic activity as water and air pollution. This conflict persists, long after we condemn and dismiss from consideration gross forms of greed and corruption and say that neither hypocrisy, incompetence, or reduced profit is what we have in mind in recommending business participation in social action.

Business is by far the most extensive and heterogeneous of all human activity. It has, even more than other areas of human activity, back alleys of self-interest in which the struggle for survival breeds desperation. It has comfortable front offices, as well, in which greed fed by success produces various forms of piracy. The rigors of competition, no less harsh for being "imperfect" in the economic sense, develop in the morally weak the temptation to cut corners and to conceal as long as possible the social costs of careless economic activity and other offenses against the public. The apparent rascality of competitors is legendary in all competitive industries, and like hypocrisy is more easily believed in than demonstrable as real. Rule breaking, falsely imputed to others, often becomes the justification for defensive departures from ethical practice. The human tendency to detect unethical behavior in others, whether demonstrable or not, is a common complication in competitive endeavors.

But the morality of the used-car lot or fraud in more elegant surroundings is not really our concern here. For even well-meaning, honest, and educated men—the conscientious professionals to whom this book is addressed— the pressure to attain profit targets quite simply tempts and sometimes compels postponement of socially directed projects more often than it prompts unethical acts. The pressures of the present at the expense of the future, the motives of the profit-center manager to win the approval of his superiors by meeting his profit commitments, the system of control of decentralized operations, and the need to satisfy quantitative measures of performance divert effort away from social problems which might otherwise be susceptible to effective but expensive attention. The predicament of every industry, varying from time to time in urgency, is essentially the same.

Because every cent devoted to charitable contribution, to support of the arts, and to investment in social problems is usually half a cent deducted from profit, the central conflict between self-interest and social concern cannot be explained away. So long as it exists, it can be used with a dash of cynicism to note that it is not easy to reconcile them nor likely that business leaders should even wish to. If we add to the difficulty of striking a balance between divergent interests the problem of establishing standards for ethical behavior in complex situations, we may conclude that those who wish to argue against corporate involvement in noneconomic activities will always have something to say. Piracy, hypocrisy, and naiveté, all deservedly unpopular, can always be alleged or detected in business activity. The very concept of profit is as ugly to many living on the margins of affluence as original sin itself.

The practical effect of the isolationist doctrine is to authorize action clearly inimical to society by companies and managers who think themselves law-abiding. Thus, the manufacture of DDT and some of its variants persists long after its cumulative harmfulness has become well-known. It is assisted by spirited attempts of manufacturers to delay the effective date of legal bans on its use. This action has a dreary history in perhaps quite honest but biased attacks upon Rachel Carson's *Silent Spring* from the moment of its first appearance. The continued discharge from 1926 to 1970 into Lake Champlain by the International Paper Company of mercury-laden sludge—even after an accumulation which would take several million dollars to remove had ruined one part of the lake and threatened it all—must have been accompanied by an extraordinarily fierce economic self-justification practiced by the honest men who run this company. Public acquiescence in such behavior, like that accompanying much traditional industrial performance, is illustrated by a 1970 petition from the village of Ticonderoga, New York, while itself discharging raw sewerage into Lake Champlain, that the mill be kept open to save the hundred jobs it provided to the villagers. That a new mill equipped to avoid pollution will not be ready to replace this old one for yet a year or two illustrates the inevitable lag between practice justifying new restrictive legislation and the perceived need for new regulation. The slowness of civic entities to correct their own abuses of the environment illustrates the general reluctance to pay the costs of unwarranted exploitation. In the meantime, International Paper, like many another member firm of this and other vulnerable industries, has announced for all its plants a $101 million four-year plan to combat pollution which will be in effect in 1974. Whether it will be required to remove its poisonous deposits from Lake Champlain remains at this writing to be seen. In retrospect, praise by Milton Friedman of classical capitalism cannot justify either company or town behavior in their destruction of priceless public property.

In the case of cigarettes, members of the isolationist school would contest vigorously the realization that smoking is foolish and dangerous, while diversifying defensively at the pace suggested by their estimate of how much time is left before the market for cigarettes is closed by law or custom. If we ask what a more responsible manufacturer might do if he were a member of the other school, we would have to say that presumably he would go out of the business as soon as possible, at a higher cost to tobacco growers, distributors, stockholders, and advertising firms than the first group would accept. The extent to which dedication to the historic economics of an industry can overcome objective evidence is strikingly illustrated by the conviction with which some manufacturers appear to repudiate the statistical validity of the data relating cigarette-smoking to cancer.

The executives of the cigarette industry's advertising agencies, themselves enrolled variously in the two schools of thought we are examining, have a much easier choice. Agencies controlled by the isolationists would accept and seek cigarette advertising and devote creative and possibly legally misleading persuasion to extending the practice of smoking. Agencies managed by social interventionists would simply refuse cigarette accounts—a decision long since taken by several. Such a decision, of course, is far less damaging to the agency than ceasing to manufacture cigarettes would be to tobacco farmers, employees, and stockholders.

(Advertising agencies, it should be noted in passing, have themselves notoriously complex problems of responsibility, no matter what the social conscience of their principals.)

The isolationist manufacturer of prescription amphetamines ("pep pills," which the Food and Drug Administration says are useful medically for only three minor needs in narcolepsy—excessive sleepiness—hyperactivity in certain children with brain damage, and for a single brief period per patient to curb appetite in the obese) continues to manufacture millions of pills which, if he is honest, he sends out only through legitimate channels. Though he knows that illicit drug traffic ultimately thrives on the surplus of production over medical need, he is disturbed not at all by the rupture in an already much criticized drug distribution system which takes amphetamines as "speed" to illegal use. He is also untroubled by the tendency of physicians to respond to promotion by prescribing amphetamines to more people and for a longer time than is medically justified. If demand is stimulated by illicit use and overprescription, he would reason, the remedy is presumably legal action and FDA clampdowns on advertising and promotion. If all drug manufacturers took this course and if finally the public became indignant about amphetamines, additional regulation, following Congressional hearings, developed without significant industry or medical cooperation, would ultimately be inevitable. All this would presumably take place in the face of the notorious failure of law enforcement to reduce traffic in certain drugs among the young.

The social interventionists might argue that in view of the actual legitimate market for amphetamines and the number of suppliers, the business should be abandoned. The leading firm in the development of this class of pharmaceuticals might elect to continue production, but revise its advertising and promotional material, and spend money investigating ways in which such products enter the drug culture. If the firm finds competitors behaving illegally, then what to do becomes so complicated as to revive one's interest in industry self-regulation. Just as the leading manufacturer of computers has without self-congratulation made a university grant of $5 million to study the impact of technology on society, so might a firm in an industry as conspicuously profitable as pharmaceuticals contribute to research on such urgent topics as the effects of drugs on the human system or the origins of drug abuse. In the short run, the firm enlisting in the ranks of the socially responsible would be penalized, but as we shall see later, it probably has strategic alternatives more lucrative and responsible to which it could transfer its technical, marketing, and financial resources. Its executives are also entitled to make some concessions to their self-respect.

The dangers of oversimple illustration are many. Rather than multiply examples in order to clarify the strategic consequences of alternate approaches to issues of responsibility, we should repeat that the essential difference between managers in these two camps lies in their beliefs about the functions of business and the extent to which the undesirable consequences of business activity are understood and thought to be part of the manager's planning problems. The degree to which responsibility is assumed early as a matter of conscience rather than accepted late as a matter of law makes the essential difference. This intangibility may be difficult to isolate and to trace through specific decisions, but the difference in the kind of organization it breeds and the quality of the economic contribution it offers is available to outside observers. It is clear as day to self-aware insiders.

THE CASE FOR INVOLVEMENT

It is true that the primary function of business is to create material wealth. This is a vital function, for material well-being is the basis of all other forms of wealth. It is not always honestly pursued, and self-centered activities are often passed off as something more pretentious. The technical problems of success in competition are worth full-time attention. The management of business firms, like all other walks of life, is beset by biases and shortcomings. Managers, like professors, know little outside their own fields. More importantly, social contributions cannot usually be achieved without reducing present profit, especially when espousal of controversial causes produces a backlash of boycott. Profit is essential not only to the support of all noneconomic activities, but to the survival of the corporation and crucially to the continuance of the responsible executive's own career. The sheer difficulty of managing effective involvement in social problems and of judging whether one strategy is morally or ethically superior to another will always support those who think that the business of business is simply to shape its strategy within the law with no concern but its profits.

The arguments for the active participation of corporations in public affairs and for the assumption of responsibility for the impact of economic activity upon society are nonetheless gaining ground. This 'momentum is more real than rhetorical, even given the abundance of apparently empty talk. It appears to be propelled by four fundamental ideas. The first is that *government regulation, certainly essential for the provision of ground rules for competition and the prohibition of grossly improper and dishonest behavior, is neither a subtle instrument for reconciling private and public interests nor an effective substitute for knowledgeable self-restraint.* The second proposition is that *in an industrial society corporate power, vast in potential strength, must be brought to bear on certain social problems if they are to be solved at all; it can legitimately be applied to social problems in the presence of internally generated and externally monitored safeguards.* The third proposition is that *corporate executives of the caliber, integrity, intelligence, and humanity required to run substantial companies cannot be expected to confine themselves to their narrow economic activity and to ignore its social consequences.*

This for these reasons. They are more and more attracted by the opportunity to apply corporate power to socially desirable ends; they are aware that social, political, and economic affairs are increasingly interrelated; they are at least intuitively conscious that a large "private" corporation is a public institution and that its management is conducted under the guidance of implicit moral values constituting a corporate conscience. The final proposition holds that *the dangers and problems of corporate participation in public affairs can be dealt with through research, education, government control, and self-regulation.* To each of these propositions we must give some attention.

The idea that businessmen should be relatively free of the need for self-restraint rests on the assumption that government regulation can be sufficiently specific, knowledgeable, and timely to check or forestall abuse without being damaging to initiative. We have had much experience with national regulation by the Antitrust division of the Department of Justice and the Federal Trade Commission for all industry, by the Interstate Commerce Commission, Food and Drug Administration, Securities and Exchange Commission, Civil Aeronautics Board, the Federal Power, Communications, and Maritime Commissions for specific industries, and in the various states with counterparts and extensions of these and other bodies. Besides regular surveillance of business activities by the courts and powerful administrative agencies, we have the influential hearings into industrial activity by the Congress, either through continuing series of inquiries as in the case of the drug industry or more specific investigations of the need for new regulation.

Our national experience with government regulation of business, too long a story to be retold here, should tell us that necessary as is regulation it cannot possibly design the ideal relationship between the corporation and society. The leaders of virtually every industry, as a matter of ideology and desire to exploit unchecked newly discovered opportunity, once fought all regulation as evil and wherever practical made captive in one way or another the agency assigned to regulate them. With a decline in the hostility between business and government developed during the recent history of the relationship between the Defense Department, NASA, and the Atomic Energy Commission with large-scale business, and with greater understanding in government of the problems of doing business, the present disposition of business leaders is to recognize the need for standards in such matters as drug quality, tire and automobile safety, advertising claims, and other matters in which bad practice by one firm makes good practice economically impossible for all. Even acquiescence to a simple rule-setting role for regulation has been hard to achieve, but no responsible voice commanding a following now argues that government regulation can be dispensed with. The realization that it should be designed in negotiation between lawmakers and affected industries to make it fair and effective is a recent consequence of a redirection of business interests away from evading all regulation toward seeking rules which would make ethical competition feasible.

At the same time, it is clear that new forms of regulation or effective enforcement come late to the problem, as in the case of water and air pollution. When the problems are far advanced, it is hard to design incentives and restraints equitably. They become expensive and cumbersome to administer over the protests of competitors not acceding to the justice of the regulation. The incentives and rewards for members of regulatory agencies do not bring them talent equal in most cases to their problems. Our economic system is based on the fertility of entrepreneurial initiative; we seek, therefore, to leave as much room for initiative as possible. Freedom of course includes the latitude to do wrong as well as right and is predicated more on responsibility than police power. If corporate power is to be regulated more by public law than by private conscience, a large part of our national energy will have to be spent keeping watch over corporate behavior, ferreting out problems, designing and revising detailed laws to deal with them, and enforcing those laws even as they become obsolete.

The alternative to much greater but still inadequate intervention by the state in economic affairs is for businessmen to exhibit a clear and lively sense of public obligation, a sensitivity to the social cost of their economic activity, and a willingness to punish irresponsibility in their own ranks. A manager of a paper company can, if he will, program a more satisfactory and equitable replacement of old mills providing jobs in remote communities than can an undermanned regulatory agency. The specter of regulation ill designed to produce in specific situations the delicate balance between private and public interests can be laid to rest only by a highly visible and authentic manifestation that corporate power, rather than only public law, will be effectively addressed to the problem. The principal justification for leaving corporate power unchecked is the emergence of the doctrine of social responsibility. This doctrine is the only alternative we have to an unworkable extension of the role of government in our economic system. It will of course never be prudent to rely only on the conscience of individuals, to relinquish the role of fair and sensible laws, or to suspend public criticism of business practice. But to argue that a businessman should knowingly ignore the consequences of his company's impact upon its physical and social environment until new laws are passed is in this day wantonly irresponsible in itself.

The public expectation that business will behave not only legally but with visible regard for the rights of competitors, customers, and the general public grows, then, rapidly more determined. The critics of business, once content to condemn corporate behavior in clinical ignorance on the basis of ideological assumptions alone are now testing the advertised nutritional value of foodstuffs, checking into the quality of automobile service, measuring the effectiveness of emission control devices, comparing the prices of branded and generic drugs, just as students are criticizing the relevance of their college educations and the slow pace with which the nation approaches its social problems. The only practical response to this movement is acknowledgment of its power and authority. Because the executive of today is ordinarily as sensitive as other citizens to the upgrading of our goals as a society, he is more than his predecessors willing to acquiesce. In a society as much in need of reform as present-day America, he cannot for long be told that concern for the problems of society, especially those which his company wittingly or unintentionally worsens, are none of his business.

We turn now to the second proposition underlying the present redefinition of corporate responsibility. It has become commonplace to assert that in a corporate society corporate power is necessary to solve problems beyond the reach of local and national government, of nonprofit organizations, and of individuals. In the Johnson and Nixon Administrations, the invitation to businessmen and corporations to move into the public arena has become more fervent. Corporate involvement in public issues is increasing on two fronts—educational activity as a contribution to community development and entrepreneurial ventures in needed services expected to produce some profit for the service rendered. The recently curtailed Job Corps Program and the National Alliance of Businessmen with its government support for corporate training of disadvantaged minority groups and its corporate commitment to provide jobs are small indications of a new tendency to trust corporate motives and to respect corporate competence. Suggestions that postal reform should lead in the direction of corporate organization, if not eventually detachment of the Post Office from the federal government, are beginning to show results in the postal reforms of 1970. Business has expanded its search for opportunity to devise reclamation procedures for exhaust gases, and for effluent and solid waste, entering into occasional joint research contracts as in one instance to find for utilities a practical way to recapture sulphur from the burning of fuel oil. Here, of course, the economic compulsion is to make the process feasible—e.g., at least profitable enough to justify investment in research and equipment. But the principal motive clearly is to make economical the reduction of pollution, rather than to seek profit as such. The supply of free sulphur is indeed abundant.

The entry of firms like General Electric, Time, Inc., Raytheon, Litton Industries, Westinghouse, and Xerox into education and the efforts of U. S. Gypsum, Aerojet, Lockheed, Ford, and of many other companies to rehabilitate housing, establish factories and training facilities in the ghettos similarly reflect a widespread recognition of obligation even more than a search for market opportunity. The quest to make these ventures profitable is to make them feasible, effective, and expansible, not, as is sometimes alleged, to make money out of the misfortunes of the poor.

The early efforts of corporate enterprise, with whatever combination of self-interest and public interest one wishes to impute, to find a role in problem areas where the promise of profit is not inviting have not been accorded the success optimistically expected by some. To successfully train and employ men and women who have long been prisoners of the welfare and poverty culture has proved agonizingly difficult. Joint enterprises to support black capitalism, for example, have run into economic, human, and technical problems which no one was initially prepared to handle. But despite setbacks and disillusion early innocence is being replaced by more realistic expectations. Determination replaces overoptimism.

We are experiencing a novel extension of corporate activity responsive primarily to social obligation rather than to self-interest, though of course ultimately involving both. Beneath the confusion currently obscuring this essentially natural evolution of American capitalism, business and society are tacitly redefining the role of industry in modern life. It is now in many quarters expected that corporate power and management skill should be applied in areas like vocational education, social justice, race relations, and the rehabilitation of cities and regions. This expectation implies an acceptance by business of responsibility to society accelerated by the idealism of our youth, by public inquiry into racism and injustice, and by violence in the cities. It implies also a higher level of managerial competence and morality than has hitherto been required.

The suspicion that once would have attended corporate attention to public problems is much less virulent today. The arguments that a company should pursue *only* those growth opportunities which produce the greatest profit possibility are losing force. For even the most successful company there is not much money to be made in the ghetto; the hiring of disadvantaged minority groups does not increase productivity. The need to extend the benefits of a technological-industrial system to these areas are seen as important enough to justify corporate entry. Many social problems are left unattended by medicine, the law, the church, and the schools, and are beyond the reach of legislators. They are complex enough to be worthy of the highest technical, professional, and organizational skills that business executives can muster.

The safeguarding of the public from exploitation at corporate hands has as yet been less of a problem than, for example, corruption in the disbursement of public funds by local public agencies. The visibility of corporate behavior in the community, the quality of corporate concern and its origins in conscience, and the necessity for various constituencies to be satisfied have been automatic assurance of the sincerity and integrity of most corporate efforts in public problem areas. That any public danger follows corporate involvement has so far not been demonstrated or much feared, patently because the motives of those who have led the way are not suspect. That corporations have not taken advantage of the opportunities for graft and corruption in government-supported projects is in itself a reflection of both rising standards of individual integrity and effective control.

Students of the corporation have noted with interest the transformation of this institution, in what John Brooks in *The Great Leap* calls the most striking social development since 1929, from a status suspected of ruthless wrongdoing to that of benign respectability. Under the steady improvement in the ethical level of business practice, sociologists have noted the appearance within corporations of a system of private government which regularizes and makes fair the impact upon individuals of managerial power. Philip Selznick[4], for example, finds that "due process," which in civil life goes far beyond codified law to regulate social behavior, is operative within corporations; A. A. Berle described this development as "constitutionalization." Its impact is to establish norms of what may or may not be done, to restrain actions which curtail the rights of others, and to extend to all employees, for example, the rights won by some in legitimate negotiations between management and organized labor. In corporations of some size, complexity, and visibility to the public, the need for its actions to appear fair to its mem-

---

[4]Philip Selznick, "Private Government and the Corporate Conscience," (unpublished manuscript prepared for Symposium on Business Policy, April 8-11, 1963, Harvard Business School).

bers and in fact to all its constituencies is a powerful check on the irresponsible use of private power. That some corporations may still be tangled jungles, with guerilla warfare conducted from ambush, does not obscure the trend or the inevitability that they will be better managed if they are not to decline. The reality of the corporate conscience, like that of the individual conscience, is essential to an open society valuing and permitting responsible freedom.

The third proposition, in effect that present-day corporate executives are increasingly the kind of people who cannot be expected to confine themselves to pursue economic activity while ignoring its social consequences, means merely that managers will concern themselves and their companies with social problems because they find it satisfying and stimulating to do so. It would be untactful for us to attempt to document the progress asserted in this statement through the appointments now being made to corporate high office in our leading companies. But the zest for social problems is evident not only in time spent on them by the best known of our corporate chairmen and presidents, but in the attitudes of their subordinates. Successive classes of vice presidential and presidential timber in the Advanced Management Program at the Harvard Business School reflect unmistakably accelerating appreciation of the magnitude of the problem, a realistic appraisal of the complexity of proposed solutions, and a hopeful interest in what strategic planning can do to make idealism workable.

The concern for the health of the society in which business operates leads these days to managers speaking in support of action not in the immediate interest of their companies. The Jenney Oil Company, in a series of newspaper advertisements some time ago, urged public support of rail-commuter transportation in Boston. The president of Atlantic Richfield has acknowledged the desirability of restricting the use of private automobiles on city streets. To be sure, such minor concessions to the public interest, like Henry Ford's deference to it in repeated public statements, are small recompense for the inaction over many decades of the automobile and petroleum industries in dealing with pollution by the internal combustion engine, estimated in 1970 to be the largest single cause of the air quality problem. These small but refreshing precursors of individual independence, however, may some day lead to greater involvement of business executives in the great debates underlying public policy. Of small importance in themselves, they may well authorize speaking out on the part of many men in management who would like to do so but until now have not dared.

The fear of controversy diminishes slightly, as experience shows its consequences to be less lethal than feared. Thus, the organization called "Business Executives Move for Peace in Vietnam" has enlisted since 1967 executives willing to challenge national policy and to subject themselves and their organizations to public displeasure. The members are not acting as private individuals, for their corporate affiliation is always stated forthrightly to document their qualifications as businessmen and to call attention to the importance of their opinions. Usually it is the colorful maverick, head of a small business with little to lose, who enters into controversy with a courage considered eccentric by the officers of a large corporation maintaining its neutrality for fear of offense. This organization, however, listed in 1968 such names as Harry E. Niles, chairman of the Baltimore Life Insurance Company; Max Pavlevsky, then president of Scientific (now Xerox) Data Systems; Joseph E. McDowell, president of Servomation

Corporation; and Edward Lamb, chairman of Lamb Enterprises. In late 1970 this group numbered 3,100 people, mostly officers of small and middle-sized businesses. But, according to the *New York Times* of January 3, 1971, in its membership are included George Weissman, president of Philip Morris; Roger Sonnabend, chairman of Sonesta International Hotels; Lawrence Phillips, president of Phillips-Van Heusen; and Bennett Cerf, chairman of Random House; Marriner Eccles, former chairman of the Federal Reserve Board; and J. Sinclair Armstrong, former chairman of the Securities and Exchange Commission. Speaking out on the war culminated, in a sense, with the testimony before the Senate Foreign Relations Committee on April 15, 1970 by Louis B. Lundborg, not, so far as I know, a member of BEMPV but chairman of the Bank of America. Lundborg said he considered our involvement in Vietnam a tragic national mistake of colossal proportions, morally indefensible and practically unsustainable. He said that people like him were to blame for our continued engagement in an unwise war for not speaking up and speaking out sooner.

John T. Connor, chairman of Allied Chemical Corporation, told the Business Council on May 8, 1970, that the continuation of the Vietnam War and especially the Cambodian intensification was as bad for American business as for the American people generally. Thomas J. Watson, Jr. testified on June 2, 1970 before the Senate Foreign Relations Committee against continuance of the war. Charles B. McCoy, president of DuPont, spoke out against the war to the Manufacturing Chemists Association on June 4.[5]

---

[5]The Lundborg, Connor, Watson, and McCoy statements are referred to in L. L. L. Golden's "War and Big Business," *Saturday Review,* September 12, 1970, p. 95.

Some executives feel that the corporation itself should be committed to stands on certain public issues. Thus, Joseph Wilson, then chief executive officer of the Xerox Corporation, said in 1964:[6]

The corporation cannot refuse to take a stand on public issues of major concern; failure to act is to throw its weight on the side of the status quo, and the public interprets it that way.

Peter McColough, his successor as president and chief officer of the company, has argued at annual meetings of shareholders, in support of the same view, that individuals in the company must not be prevented from expressing dissenting views so that the corporation does not override their liberty. Similarly, he believes that if all corporations were to take forthright stands on public issues, the variety of opinions would be as great as among individuals, and the public would be protected from overpowerful influence on public opinion of a few powerful firms. If he were to be deprived of the privilege of stating publicly his views on controversial questions or to contribute to an official corporation position on the same issues, he would lose interest in continuing to be an executive. Both Wilson and McColough have told their stockholders in effect that if they do not approve they should either dismiss their management or sell their stock. Ownership of Xerox stock, over time, has been extremely profitable for investors.

Whatever the problems of official corporate positions on controversial issues not directly related to the corporation's own interests may be, the improvement in the lawful, ethical, and humane quality of corporate practice

---

[6]Quoted in Learned, Christensen, Andrews, and Guth, *Business Policy: Text and Cases,* p. 532.

during the last 70 years is in any case quite unmistakable. From close at hand the rate of progress, subject in definition to contentious subjectivity, is harder to realize. Improvement can be directly traced to the aspirations of men moving into top management positions and their sensitivity to public opinion.

Companies choose for positions of top leadership the best men they can find and have the wit to recognize. For years such men were the typical product of the technology upon which their businesses were based. They had learned the hard way how to make technical progress profitable. "This technological world," writes Philip Sporn, himself an engineer and the retired head of American Electric Power Company and the Ohio Valley Electric Corporation, "is, in its final evaluation, a world created by the engineers. Its successes, but also its failures, all are the product of the engineers. Thus in the important sense the pollution problems we are suffering from today represent a failure of engineers and a bankruptcy of engineering."[7] The realization grows that we need top managers with the ability to transcend what Eli Goldston, president of Eastern Gas and Fuel Associates, calls the "human limits of technology—the problems of persuasion and decision, limited not by science and mathematics and engineering but limited by our ability to understand the problems of our society and to assemble the necessary public support behind the solutions."[8] Observation of the selection process for chief executive does not justify announcing the millennium, for the top responsibility in

---

[7]From "Technology, Environment, Morality and Ethics in the World of Today and Tomorrow," An Honors College Lecture delivered April 15, 1970 at Wesleyan University, p. 10.

[8]From "The Limits of Technology," a Diebold Lecture delivered at the Harvard Business School, November 7, 1969, p. 20.

large corporations still outruns the average of capability brought to it. But the need for breadth of imagination in recognizing opportunity, for the capacity to change objectives and policy in the face of changing opportunity, for the self-knowledge required to gauge corporate resources and the market opportunities to which they might be applied, and for the sensitivity to win organization support in the company human and political system is beginning to produce the kind of leader whose motivations are not those of the economic isolationist, pursuing his own gain with a steely-eyed disregard for the future of his company or of its society.

As the levels of formal education rise and the professionalization to which I will allude later continue to advance, executives will turn to social problems as concerned individuals simply because they want to. In recognition of their motives and capability, their participation generally will be allowed and welcomed. A concerned individual who is president of a substantial corporation cannot act apart from it even if he would; he must bring at least the prestige of his firm with him. To enlist its power by designing its strategy to encompass a chosen set of social conditions is only a second small step. The problem of bringing together personal and corporate aspirations for a better world are attractive because to men who are intelligent as well as concerned they are intellectually stimulating. To populate an organization with younger people who are also intelligent and concerned becomes easier and henceforth will probably be possible only if the stated objectives and observable behavior of the organization include more than self-preservation and meeting the economic needs of its customers and employees.

The prohibition against such interests and activities left over from the laissez-faire doctrine of Adam Smith and fostered still by the suspicious theorists who postulate in effect venality and self-aggrandizement as the primary motives for economic activity becomes less compelling. The person humane, intelligent, and experienced enough to be a general manager at high level in a complex company will join the interventionists' ranks, then, because it is the natural and obvious thing to do. Two conditions only make it necessary to defend his presence: an obsolete set of arguments based on a hostile definition of the role of business in society; and the presence in high office still of narrowly educated men making intuitive strategic decisions out of technical tradition, jungle instincts of conduct, skill in emergency improvisations, and a vague loyalty to the self-vindicating economic rationale offered to them. A new kind of manager has been emerging from the process of education and natural selection.

The best executives of today's leading corporations, as I have occasion to know from a considerable acquaintance with many of them, are men of stature and integrity. Those who have risen above the most common problem of their position—overwork—share the concerns of the age in which they live and they wish to leave some impact upon it. Although convention and corporate routine have largely kept these men from making use of their opportunity, they are already breaking their bonds and taking their place with the leaders of other professions in service to society.

The fourth proposition supporting the participation of companies in social problems is mostly an assurance that such activity, conducted by the kind of generalists we are making way for, is neither impractical nor dangerous. The competence to deal with the social consequences of strategic decision can be nurtured through education, experience, and proper selection; it is integrally part of the unitary capacity for strategic planning. The other professions, including law and medicine, distinguished by individual achievement and fully authorized to deal in social problems, are not so far ahead that they are out of sight.

Every profession, to be sure, is subject to capture by complacency with its own achievements or conventions about what is practical or possible. In recent years each one has been shaken by its younger members to reconsider its premises. The corporate conscience, the inexorable clarification of due process supporting social justice within the corporation as well as in society at large, the new muscularity of government regulation, signs of industry self-regulation, the revitalization of boards of directors, and the availability of criticism from a pluralism of standards and prejudices in an open society are all available to contain corporate power wrongly directed. Since this is a book on how to perform general management effectively and responsibly, we must press forward on the assumption that business leaders will prove equal to what is required of them. The quality of leadership available to the citizenry in other walks of life does not suggest that the average will be lowered by corporate executives. Up to this point, in fact, society has been needlessly deprived of the participation of some of its best qualified members.

THE CATEGORIES OF CONCERN

Two major questions remain. What is the range of corporate involvement available to a company? What considerations should guide its choice of opportunity? The problems affecting the quality of life in the society to which the company belongs may usefully be thought of as extending through a set of spheres from the firm itself to the world community. The sheer extent of social and environmental problems grows rapidly under the impetus of two major developments which promise to dominate the 1970s. The first of them is the hitherto unforeseen consequences of technological advance and industrial growth. The second is a feeling of urgency, fed by but not confined to environmental faddism, sweeping through a press and public newly alarmed and indignant. The effect of this combination of increased knowledge and higher action priorities is to pose, once again, as in the case of proliferating market opportunity, the need for strategic choice and criteria to transform that choice from an intuitive to a reasoned decision.

To begin with the problems of the world society, of immediate interest principally to firms in multinational business, the opportunity to contribute to industrialization in underdeveloped nations falls within the economic responsibilities of business. The willingness to undertake joint ventures rather than insist on full ownership, to share management and profits in terms not immediately related to the actual contributions of other partners, to cooperate otherwise with governments looking for alternatives to capitalism, to train nationals for skilled jobs, to enter businesses to meet social as well as material needs, to reconcile different codes of ethical practice in matters of taxes and bribery, illustrate the opportunity for combining entrepreneurship with responsibility. The potential for peace and economic development makes East-West trade under some conditions as much an issue of responsibility as of economic return. A relatively simple example of enlightened world practice is the automobile industry's support of free trade in the face of effective competition from foreign imports. The economic justification for this in terms of freedom to export or as a bid for freedom to conduct operations abroad is relevant, but not enough to determine the decision. Larger issues than the immediate prosperity of the affected firm are at stake.

When Adriano Olivetti determined that his company should manufacture as well as market in the United States, it was for the reason that he believed a world company should make the kind of contribution to even a developed economy that marketing operations carried as a responsibility with them. Unilever, and some other world companies, have undertaken businesses in Africa and elsewhere not because they wanted to, but because as trusted participants in the economy of the country, the local government wanted them to. The move to share knowhow, undertake management contracts, accept minority positions, establish research and manufacturing facilities abroad, are illustrative of the maturing of world corporations into fully contributing institutions. That profits result, or would in the long term not otherwise be accumulated or repatriated and that permission to operate in certain countries can be obtained or kept in no other way do not necessarily affect the quality of the motivation we are considering. The world corporation that survives and grows in the world now unfolding will tend to be sensitive to local needs and to enter into a variety of businesses, activities, and organization forms for reasons other than their prominence in the rank-order list of profitable projects. That in the long run enlightened practice and maximum profitability converge appears better established, interestingly enough, in international than in domestic business.

Within the United States, problems susceptible to some constructive attention from business firms occur in virtually every walk of life. The choice of how to participate is here bewilderingly large. A firm would most naturally begin with the environmental consequences of its manufacturing processes or the impact of its product upon the public. Thus, Charles F. Jones, president of the Humble Oil and Refining Company—the American subsidiary of the Standard Oil Company of New Jersey—chose in 1970 the pollution issue as one in which a clear distinction would be made between responsible and irresponsible business. Within the objective that his industry's "use of land, air, and water does not detract from their usefulness to other subsequent users," he finds an expensive list[9] of consequences paralleled in most heavy industry. Included are the elimination of oil field brines from surface streams and creekbeds, the cleanup of areas where accident or irresponsible practice has scarred the land, the elimination of smoke and smell from refining operations and of transfer losses during distribution operations, the disposition of automotive crankcase drainings without use of public sewers, the discovery of presently unknown ways in which oil operations may be affecting the environment, and attention to other problems created by consumer use of oil products, including development of a fuel for pollution-free automobiles.

A company must first put its house in order or embark upon a long program to make it so. It may then take interest or even find economic opportunity in other public problems, either within the context of philanthropic contribution or through business operations which in essence seek out proper economic opportunity in social need. It may take part in education from elementary and vocational levels to higher education, in esthetics and support of the arts by purchasing paintings and sculpture and the use of architecture in producing attractive as well as

[9]See *The Humble Way,* Second Quarter 1970, a publication of the Humble Oil and Refining Company, p. 18.

functional buildings, in politics through corporate participation in discussion of national issues and in taking positions, or in encouragement of individual participation in
political processes, in problems of social justice like race
relations and equal opportunity for women, in society's
logistical problems like transportation, trash disposal,
noise abatement, and in even larger issues like the impact
upon society of technological change. Once corporate
concern for such national problems is recognized as
legitimate, it is not hard to find problems to work on. The
question becomes which ones.

A third category of concern is filled by the problems of
the communities in which the company operates. These
constitute principally the urban manifestation of the national problems already referred to—inadequate housing,
unemployment in the poverty culture, substandard medical care, ineffective education, rampant ugliness, transportation tieups, and the like. The city has become the
special focus of our national decay; it appeals to companies as the proper arena for economic and social action
because of its nearness and its compactness. The difficulties of learning how to take effective action are correspondingly grave. For philanthropic purposes, the near
community is obviously the corporation's favored opportunity, for the development of such mutually beneficial
projects as vocational training and adequate housing
come close to supporting the economic purposes of the
business. Business cannot remain healthy in a sick community; ultimately no corporation is an island.

Because the city has quite naturally become the corporation's special concern, we find many ventures addressed to its problems. Thus, recognition of the ghetto
has led to voluntary efforts at training sponsored by the
private Urban Coalition and the government-business

partnership in the National Alliance of Businessmen. The Watts Manufacturing Company subsidiary of Aerojet making tents and crates in the first urban riot zone to capture national attention, the AVCO printing plant in Roxbury, the Kodak and Xerox sponsorship of black businesses in Rochester were early illustrations of the opportunity for self-supporting economic activity in hitherto arid areas. In their subsequent history these ventures have taught us the great difficulties inherent in taking single steps to recast a culture. The systems which must be altered to make such enterprises workable are still little understood.

Attempts to supply housing, supported by ingenious rehabilitation ventures of U.S. Gypsum and by the billion-dollar pledge of the insurance industry to sponsor developments eligible for rent subsidy, have also been beset by the difficulties of altering one aspect of a social system without being ready to cope with the impact of the change upon the total system. Assistance to education and attention to logistical problems, like trash compaction and disposal, have attracted hundreds of company interventions. The art of dealing with local governments and school boards is one that has to be acquired; inexperience on both sides has delayed progress.

It is probable that the problems of the city will continue to dominate the social action of corporations and that a gradually increasing sophistication will make it more effective than it has been so far. A National Industrial Conference Board study in 1968 (*Business Amid Urban Crisis*) surveyed the involvement of 356 firms, 80 percent of which reported that they expected their urban activity to increase. No company reported planning reduced activity. The chairman of PPG Industries, Robinson F. Barker, who has had bitter experience in Roxbury,

reported the mixture of motivations prompting such intervention:[10]

Motivations for our involvement include both self-interest
and public interest—to make a dollar, to expand a market,
to realize a return on an investment, to sell more goods; and,
to stop the riots, to save our cities, to protect life and property, to halt deterioration, to reclaim the American dream,
to achieve a social order based on justice and opportunity for
all. Each of us can pick the labels that are most appealing
personally, but we must not expect effective action to flow
from reliance on either self-interest or public interest alone.
The problem is too complicated for simple answers or simple
motives.

We must not think of public interest motivations as sheer
altruism, but rather as enlightened self-interest. Looking at
the question negatively, what chance is there for free enterprise and democracy if the riots don't stop, if the cities cannot be saved, and if we cannot achieve a social order consistent with our ideals?

An interesting early study of how firms actually make
a decision to enter into urban affairs has been completed
as a doctoral thesis by Patrick T. Jesaitis. Examination of
the decision process indicates that in the three firms
studied pressure was exerted upon the top executives of
the community by the existence of federal government
programs and by their own personal values. "Their combined force increases until it reaches a point when the
top executive decides that his firm must engage in some
activity as a response thereto. The executive initiates a
study of the alternatives open to the corporation and as-
signs the task to a planning group of high-ranking managers, reserving certain decision responsibilities for him-

---

[10]*Business Amid Urban Crisis,* Studies in Public Affairs, No. 3, p. 67.

self—whether to become involved, approach to be taken, type of product or service, and size of project. The formulation of strategy related to a specific project is incomplete [because of] management's impression that the top executive is committed to act regardless of the profit implications."[11]

Moving from world to country to city takes us through the full range of social, political, and technical issues which engage the attention of corporate strategists who wish to factor social responsibility into their planning. Two other less obvious avenues of action should be considered—the industry or industries in which the company operates and the quality of life within the company itself. Every industry, like every profession, has problems which arise from a legacy of indifference, from the attitudes and stresses engendered by vigorous competition, and from the real or imagined impossibility of certain forms of interfirm cooperation under the antitrust laws. For the company which would like to raise the standards of performance in the industry there is the problem of control of its own individuals, who ignoring or disbelieving the sincerity of headquarters policy may choose or be driven to dishonest or overhucksterish behavior. But beyond this universal human problem, every industry has chronic problems of its own, like safety, quality, pricing, and pollution in which only cooperative action can effectively pick up where regulation leaves off.

The whole field of self-regulation, which becomes important as businessmen turn to responsibility as a means of preserving their assigned franchise and their freedom, has been little explored. Several industries have adopted

---

[11]From the abstract of the thesis entitled "Corporate Strategies and the Urban Crisis: A Study of Business Response to a Social Problem," unpublished thesis deposited in Baker Library, Harvard Business School.

codes of behavior, for example the cigarette industry (to influence advertising), the National Association of Broadcasters (to govern programming), and the motion picture producers (to classify the suitability of films for various audiences). Many more exhort each other usefully and otherwise at annual meetings and in seminars. But the approach to offenders is skittish and penalties for violation are almost unheard of. The force of industry opinion quietly brought to bear on the industry's more shoddy practices is slow and uncertain and does not lessen much the damage done to an entire industry by its less responsible members. Because "nice guys" are afraid of finishing last, because moralistic criticism of successful competition is bad taste, and do-goodism is generally abhorred, the power of norms of acceptable conduct is considerably diluted within the industry organization. The strategy of any firm in a roughly competitive industry must include a determination of how the industry's organization can be used or altered to raise the level of responsibility of most of its members. The personality, character, and power of a few corporation presidents, each sensitive to the ethical quality of the company and industry he is in, can be most important as they come together for industry meetings and talk in private among themselves about matters which are quite legally subject to concerted concern.

The illegality of restraint of trade and the inbred self-serving of tight guilds suggest caution in speculating about the future course of self-regulation. As the pressures of external regulation and intraindustry conscience intensify, it is not farfetched, however, to visualize industrial trade associations with established elected or appointed umpires given the staff and the power to codify behavior in sensitive areas and to discipline violations, either with publicity, or fines, or various forms of ostracism. Just as companies have established vice presidents to coordinate and plan new action on environmental problems, so industries like the pharmaceutical, automobile, and oil groups, could quite legally in their already active industry councils set up organized inquiry for identifying areas of concern, establishing objectives and standards, planning defensive and offensive strategies, and reviewing industry progress. The skill with which in the past lobbies have been made effective could well be enlarged and turned to the extension of enlightened self-interest to officially identified problems of the industry. Industry monitoring of responsibility would need outside counsel and even devil's advocates to give it courage and the perspective of objectivity, just as effective boards need independent outside directors. No better evidence of responsible concern for the protection of its own freedom and of the public's interests would be available than a less gingerly approach to private criticism of an industry by its own leaders. Industry leaders may as orators acknowledge their own problems and promise to take action, but until they organize behind the scenes to influence each other, nothing important will happen. It is economically impossible in a highly competitive industry to market products of decent quality priced to cover the full social cost of their production against products plausible in superficial quality but inherently unsafe and subsidized in resources like air and water neither paid for nor returned in kind.

Within the firm itself, free from the antitrust problems of organizing proper forms of cooperation among competitors, a company has open opportunity for satisfying its management's aspirations toward responsibility. The quality of any company's present strategy, for example, is probably always subject to improvement, as new technology and higher aspirations work together. But besides such important tangible matters as the quality of goods and services being offered to the public and the maintenance and improvement of ordinary craftsmanship, there are three other areas which in the future will become much more important than they seem now. The first of these is the review process set up to estimate the quality of top-management decision. The second is the impact upon individuals of the control systems and other organization processes installed to secure results. The third is a recognition of the role of the individual in the corporation.

The everyday pressures bearing on decisions about what to do and how to get it done make almost impossible the kind of detached self-criticism which is essential to the perpetuation of responsible freedom. The opportunity to provide for systematic review sessions becomes more explicit and self-conscious. At any rate, as a category of concern, how a management can maintain sufficient detachment to estimate without self-deception the quality of its management performance is as important as any other. The proper role of the board of directors in performing this function—long since lost sight of—requires revitalization.

The caliber and strategic usefulness of a board of directors will nonetheless remain the option of the chief executive who usually determines its function. How much he uses his board for the purposes of improving the quality of corporate strategy and planning turns, as usual, on the sincerity of his interest and his skill. Recent research has illuminated the irresponsibility of inaction in the face of problems requiring the perspective available only to properly constituted boards. This organization resource is available to general managers who recognize dormancy as waste and seek counsel in cases of conflicting responsibility.

The effective provision by a board of responsible surveillance of the moral quality of a management's strategic decisions means that current stirrings of concern about conflicts of interest will soon result in the withdrawal from boards of bankers representing institutions performing services to the company, of lawyers (in some instances) representing a firm retained by the company, and other suppliers or customers, as well as more scrupulous attention to present regulations about interlocking interests. As much attention will soon be given to avoiding the possibility of imputing conflict of interest to a director as to avoiding the actual occurrence. Stronger restrictions on conflict of interest will also affect employees of the firm, including the involvement of individuals with social-action organizations attacking the firm.

Secondly, the ethical and economic quality of an organization's performance is vitally affected by its control system, which inevitably leads people, if it is effective at all, to do what will make them look good in the terms of the system rather than what their opportunities and problems, which the system may not take cognizance of, actually require. We will examine the unintended consequences of control and measurement systems when we come to the implementation of corporate strategy; in the meantime we should note that unanticipated pressures to act irresponsibly may be applied by top management who would deplore this consequence if they knew of it. The process of promotion by which persons are moved from place to place so fast that they do not develop concern for the problems of the community in which they live or effective relationships within which to accomplish anything unintentionally weakens the participation of executives in community affairs. The tendency to measure executives in divisionalized companies on this year's profits reduces sharply their motivation to invest in social action with returns over longer times. Lifelong habits of neutrality and noninvolvement eventually deprive the community, in a subtle weakening of its human resources, of executive experience and judgment. Executive cadres are in turn deprived of real-life experience with political and social systems which they ultimately much need.

The actual quality of life in a business organization turns most crucially on how much freedom is accorded to the individual. Certainly most firms consider responsibility to their members a category of concern as important as external constituencies. It is as much a matter of enlightened self-interest as of responsibility to provide conditions encouraging the convergence of the individual's aspirations with those of the corporation, to provide conditions for effective productivity, and to reward employees for extraordinary performance.

With the entry of the corporation into controversial areas comes greater interest on the part of organization members to take part in public debate. It becomes possible for individuals to make comments on social problems that could be embarrassing to the corporation. It is at best difficult to balance the freedom of the individual and the consequences of his participation in public affairs against the interests of the corporation. The difficulty is increased if the attitudes of management, which are instinctively overprotective of the corporation, are harsh and restrictive. Short-run embarrassments and limited criticism from offended groups—even perhaps a threatened boycott—may be a small price to pay for the continued productivity within the corporation of men whose interests are deep enough and broad enough to cause them to take stands on public issues. The degree to which an organization is efficient, productive, creative, and capable of development is dependent in large part on the maintenance of a climate in which the individual does not feel suppressed, and in which a kind of freedom (analogous to that which the corporation enjoys in a free enterprise society) is permitted as a matter of course. Overregulation of the individual by corporate policy is no more appropriate internally than overregulation of the corporation by government. On the other hand, personal responsibility is as appropriate to individual liberty as corporate responsibility is to corporate freedom.

What the corporate strategist has before him to be concerned with, then, ranges from the most global of the problems of world society to the uses of freedom by a single person in his firm. The problems of his country, community, and industry lying between these extremes make opportunity for social contribution exactly coextensive with the range of economic opportunity before him. The problem of choice may be met in the area of responsibility in much the same way as in product-market combinations and in developing a program for growth and diversification.

The strategist who is sensitive to this range of issues soon concludes that there are in summary three reasons for examining the impact of his policy choices upon the public good. The first in importance is his professional concern for legality, fairness, and decency—his professional contempt for returns improperly or unfairly secured. The second is his humane concern for the progress of society and his perception of the proper uses of corporate power in dealing with problems not directly related to his present business. The third is the threat of regulation that will be ultimately forthcoming if business behavior does not meet the standards applied to it by society. Men of conscience will be concerned with their public responsibilities because they choose to be. Others will be concerned because they must be. The business firm, as an organic entity meaningfully related to its environment, must be as adaptive to demands for responsible behavior as for economic service. Special satisfaction and prestige, if not economic rewards, are available for companies which are not merely ingeniously adaptive but take the lead in shaping the moral and ethical environment within which their primary economic function is performed. Such firms are more persuasive than others, moreover, in convincing the public of the inherent impossibility in business of satisfying completely all the conflicting claims made upon it.

Conflict of Responsibilities

Once it is established that the firm must take into account the legitimate interests of other segments of society, the problem is far from solved. The already complex process of formulating a strategy capable of balancing economic opportunity, corporate resources, and personal and organizational aspirations is complicated now by an additional dimension. Furthermore, though right and wrong may be easy to determine in cases where all good lies on one side and all harm on the other, in most cases obligation to society may lead in several different directions. In some of these instances, determination of the proper course of action is acutely complex. The basic problem is the variety of interests which must be harmonized, the range of insistent and sometimes shrill definitions of rights and justice, and the conflict among legitimate claims.

The professional manager of a large, publicly held corporation is clearly in some sense responsible to the owners of his business, to its employees, to its suppliers and customers, and even to his competitors—since he owes it to them to compete "fairly." He is also responsible in some ways to certain institutions, including the local government and community, the national government and community, and the fraternity of businessmen with which he identifies himself. It is clear at once that if the interests of any one of these groups are pursued exclusively, the interests of the others will suffer. It is clear also that the stockholder interest, which was once thought to be dominant, is no longer of unchallenged primacy. Indeed, in the publicly held corporation, it is not even particularly insistent. Conventions as to what constitutes a fair dividend in relation to market price are fairly well observed. When return does not meet the individual needs of an investor, his recourse is, as we have seen, to make other investment choices. Conventions governing the extent to which other interests must be considered exist but are less clearly defined. Often the executive finds himself in situations in which it is impossible to reconcile the legitimate claims of everyone concerned. For example, there is frequently a need to move an obsolescent plant from a town that is economically dependent upon its payroll. Once such a problem has been allowed to arise, it is almost impossible to solve it without damage to some interests.

THE RESOLUTION OF CONFLICTING RESPONSIBILITY

Since the validity of strategic decision rests upon its uniqueness in combining opportunity, resources, desire, and responsibility, it is almost useless to produce generalization about how responsibility may be factored into the process. Some attention to this problem, however, may be helpful. Under a tentative national policy to increase peaceful trade with the Soviet Union and its satellites, the State Department encouraged first Goodyear and then Firestone in 1965 to accede to a request by Romania that a synthetic rubber plant be built in that country. The venture appeared to offer opportunity for satisfactory return, a broader international operation, and a contribution to strengthened ties with countries growing restless in their relations with Russia. The Goodyear Company refused the invitation on grounds of patriotism and made public its reasons. The Young Americans for Freedom took up the conservative patriotic line announced by Goodyear and threatened to picket Firestone's stores. Firestone's choice was evidently to cooperate in an experimental liberalization of national policy or to capitulate to conservative wrath. The decision to withdraw from negotiations must have been affected by its estimate of the damage to its reputation in retail stores which the YAF efforts, in effect, abetted by the largest company in its industry, threatened to bring about. It is quite possible that short-run criticism was allowed to outweigh longer term returns, but the context of the decision is not fully known. In any case, the rubber industry, dominated by a strategy dictated by Goodyear which makes original equipment business virtually profitless, was not at the time strategically ready to undertake sensitive international problems of responsibility involving East-West trade. Tire quality, safety, and pricing offered ample room for responsible innovation perhaps more than patriotism by itself could occupy.

On the other hand, when Xerox, a firm not closely pursued by competition and till now blessed with margins unavailable under any strategy in the rubber industry, was made the target of many thousands of letters inspired by the John Birch Society for its support of a series of television programs describing and implicitly approving of the nonpolitical activities of the United Nations, it did not expect to be hurt much and did not fear to pay the price—despite the business loss of some substantial accounts. Similarly, when it sponsored a program on Israel, it in effect gave up its business in the Arab countries. Although many companies have been led to make this choice, it is not ordinarily welcomed.

The necessity to compromise earnings has to be faced unless a company is to confine itself to bland courses universally accepted and safe. The risks of controversy are like the risks of market development. That cost is incurred and that mistakes about their magnitude are possible does not make involvement in controversy impractical. To be silent in a situation where change is needed is to withdraw support from social progress. When such noninvolvement is not representative of the true convictions of the management, the company is misunderstood and the opportunity for a distinctive contribution to a change considered desirable is lost. An entry should then be made in the ledgers of those who are accumulating evidence of the parasitism of the corporation upon society and of the facelessness of the supposedly heartless automatons who run them without regard for the health and well-being of society.

In concrete situations it is possible to manage choice of issues upon which to take a position with a prudent containment of risk. Controversy should in any case not be sought for its own sake, but it should be suffered if it is essential to announcement and pursuit of the strategy. When the Birmingham subsidiary of U.S. Steel called

Tennessee Coal and Iron patiently pursued for years the attempt to overcome union and popular resistance to opening jobs to blacks, it was considered skillful and courageous by some and hopelessly slow by others. In its own community it was proceeding against a social resistance almost unmovable until the enactment of legislation requiring nondiscrimination of government contractors and the 1962 labor contract permitting enactment of a policy existing on paper for all of the 20th century to date. This accomplished, the company then encountered the criticism of *The New York Times* for not using its "economic power" to speed integration and of various liberals for not exercising more leadership in an enterprise in which many other firms were doing far less. Its decision had been a deliberate deference to the explosive nature of Birmingham's feelings about integration in the matter of timing, but not in the matter of substance and ultimate result. Criticism cannot be avoided in this area and need not be feared, hindsight indicates, as much as it has been.

The choice of avenues in which to participate will of course be influenced by the personal values of the managers making the decision. In the absence of powerful predispositions, it appears appropriate to choose issues most closely related to the economic strategy of the company, to the expansion of its markets, to the health of its immediate environment, and to its own industry and internal problems. The extent of involvement relates importantly to the resources available. A company struggling to avoid bankruptcy will omit contributions to the United Fund and all other good causes. A company easily able to meet its dividend and growth-in-earnings targets can be more generous not only in its support of education and other acceptable causes but to national and world issues not directly related to its economic function. What its competence in such areas might be is open to question. The question is so serious as to suggest a principle that a company should not venture into good works that are not strategically related to its present and prospective economic functions.

As in the case of personal values and individual idiosyncrasy, a company may make well-meant decisions erratically related to nonstrategic motives. However noble these may be, they are not made strategic by good intentions. A company may make large contributions to X university because its president went there, with little or no contributions to colleges of the several vice presidents and to those of lesser alumni. It might better develop a pattern for educational support that blends the company's involvement in the educational system, its acknowledged specific debt for the contribution of technical or managerial education to the company, or reflection of the company's estimate of the resources it might properly devote to education in the light of its relevance to the company's needs or its management's appraisal of society's needs. Thus, a chemical company with a plant in a large city which runs a vocational training program for the National Alliance of Businessmen, supports the engineering school which produces many of its mechanical and chemical engineers, pays the tuition of its employees who continue their education at night, and makes substantial grants to the chemistry departments of a small number of universities conducting research ultimately related to the company's technology can relate its application of resources to its economic strategy. Although the amount to be given may be arbitrarily determined and may vary, it can over time constitute a steady contribution to an area of education geographically and technically important to the company. With many different companies making choices appropriate to their situations, pluralism in educational support should prevent its being unnaturally skewed.

What makes participation in public affairs strategic rather than improvisatory is (as we have seen in conceiving an economic strategy) a definition of objectives taking all other objectives into account and a plan which reflects the company's definition of itself not only as an economic entity but as a responsible institution in its society. When Jay Monroe of the Tensor Corporation took advertisements in *The New York Times* to announce withdrawal of the account of his publicly owned company from the Chase Manhattan Bank (in denunciation of David Rockefeller's alleged support of oil industry interests in representing to the President that the interests of the Arab nations were being too much discounted), he seemed to be acting, as he would doubtless acknowledge, as a passionate ally of Israel rather than a corporation president. His special interest in a just settlement in the Middle East obviously rose from his Jewish heritage—not from the strategy of his company. If personal passions are to dictate, rather than influence, choice of corporate involvement in public affairs, then corporate participation can become an unreasonable projection of what an individual should be doing in his own name.

When Peter Widdrington, president of Lucky Breweries, Inc., announced that his company was ready to recycle all its bottles and cans and offered, without raising its prices or deposits, to pay a cent for every no-return bottle and half a cent for every used can, he addressed himself to the environmental concern most urgent for distributors of consumer products. The economic feasibility of his recycling programs, if further confirmed, together with the community concerns with waste in the West Coast communities in which his products are sold, should make this decision strategic in its impact upon long-run success against competition. At least it is not quixotic, unrelated to technical competence, or trivial in its impact upon the social problem it addresses.

Although no body of doctrine has yet emerged to regulate the choice of issues with which a corporation might identify itself, we have made a small beginning here. When the margins within which a company operates allow it, a company should make full use of the tax deductibility, through contributions, from which it expects no direct return. The choice of worthy causes should relate to the company's concept of itself and thus at least indirectly to its economic mission. It need not be narrow or literal-minded in its tracing the connection between its own contributions to its community by including the hospital and excluding the symphony orchestra, but it should have a strategy for support of community institutions as explicit as its economic strategy or its decisions as to the kind of organization it intends to be and the kind of people it intends to enroll in its membership.

When a company goes beyond the conventional contributions of money to traditional charities and looks to the special needs of the community not being supported elsewhere, it must enter into this innovation with the same questions about its resources and competence that new product-market combinations inspire. A recreation center in the nearest ghetto may be a great need, but if the company does not have experience in this field or does not know how to secure the kind of people who do, the investment of money may come to nothing. In good works as in new markets, opportunity without the competence to develop it is a trap. Deliberate concentration on limited objectives with a plan for developing the necessary competence is infinitely preferable to scattering short-lived enthusiasm across the community's total need.

It is appropriate for any company to examine the fairness with which it makes employment opportunity available. Thus, the determined effort to retrain, train, and place minority group members in compliance with both law and conscience becomes a near-at-hand responsibility. Early efforts in this area may lead naturally to moves designed to improve the economic life of more workers than the company could hire—as in joint manufacturing ventures, support of biracial banks, and rehabilitation of housing, or other possibilities falling within the capabilities of the company. The history of naive and ineffective urban action, and the discovery of how massively difficult are the problems of the city suggest the urgent need of acquiring competence before or along the path of its involvement.

When a company looks about for new opportunity in public need, it does well to begin close to home and to move methodically into the discovery of the management capability needed. It should deal first, as a matter of obvious fairness, with the environmental pollution for which it may be responsible. The budgets and time required for this are so great that while this first task is being accomplished other smaller programs can go forward. But to buy off criticism of the sludge in the lake with scholarships for local blacks is improper and ineffective. The two programs must be unified by an understood pattern of time-phased purpose.

With a program designed for dealing with the company's adverse contributions to the environment and for insuring the fairness of its own employment practices, the company can then turn to other combinations of need, opportunity, and corporate capability that have promise in enlisting the interest of executives and in being effective in the community. If the company has only one city or region to be concerned about, it can rank the needs observed against its own capabilities and again rank the prospects for making proposed contributions economically effective. For the richest corporation the time comes when philanthropy must give way to economic performance and successful entrepreneurship must be joined with responsible concern if corporate power is to have important impact.

Without knowing opportunity, a company's resources, the values of its managers, and its aspirations to responsibility, I cannot specify the outcome of strategic planning in this or any other area. The range open to practical imagination is enormous; some strategy is required to confine it to proper proportion, to make it compatible with corporate strengths, and to relate it to programmed results.

A firm needs, then, a budget for contributions and a strategy for economic-social enterprises related to its basic business. It must approach the extension of its economic strategy into the arena of responsibilities, with the same conceptual interest in objectives and policy as in strictly economic calculations. The outcome will be influenced by the values, personal philosophy, and moral standards of the men making decisions: exercise in thinking about these issues appears to bring clarification to what remains otherwise beneath the surface of debate. A man will be as responsible as he has to be but more importantly as he wants to be. As we have seen, what he wants may change and as lesser needs are satisfied, higher needs claim attention.

PROFESSIONALIZATION OF MANAGEMENT PRACTICE

The extent to which social responsibility as a category of purpose is consciously considered and weighted is propelling the gradual professionalization of the practice of management.[12] The importance of this development, which is influential enough to examine here, is that it will soon put an end to such cliches as the businessman's *first* obligation is to his stockholders (and after that in time probably already up, responsible to other claimants). With competence increasingly considered to include social responsibility and with the concept of corporate strategy available to reconcile divergent purposes, the culture in which an executive moves is going to take him in the direction of responsibility whether he consciously wills it or not.

To evaluate the professional quality of any occupation (law, medicine, and teaching, for example), we must give attention to five hallmarks of a profession: (1) the kind of disciplined knowledge upon which practice is based, (2) the importance of the complex problems of major concern for organized society to which it is competently applied, (3) the degree of self-control by which members of the profession set standards and criticize improper behavior, (4) the respect, authority, and considerable freedom granted by the community in recognition of the work of the profession, and (5) the degree to which the practicing professional is motivated less by his own aggran-

---

[12]See Kenneth R. Andrews, "Toward Professionalism in Business Management," *Harvard Business Review,* March-April, 1969, pp. 49–60.

dizement than by the desire to satisfy needs, solve problems, or accomplish goals appropriate to his field. The
material rewards of successful performance are not valued
primarily as ends in themselves.

Obviously, not all business activity can be considered
professional. But what has happened to management
practice in recent years suggests at least that it is moving
toward professionalization. The knowledge upon which
it is based is available in professional schools in a curriculum comprising the study of "(a) functions like marketing, production, and finance which cut across all industries; (b) the organization processes like quantitative
analysis, control, and organizational behavior which cut
across all functions; (c) the social, economic, political,
and technical environmental forces affecting the individual firm; and (d) the policy processes leading to the formulation and achievement of purposes."[13] So far, certi-
fication, especially important in medicine and law, has
not seemed necessary in business, for organization safeguards and the rigors of the marketplace deal with incompetence.

Certainly this knowledge is applied to practical problems of major concern to mankind, for a material standard
of living freeing people from drudgery is vital to all human happiness and achievement. So far as community
sanction goes, business is much criticized and corporate
practice is now a favorite target of revolutionaries. But
generally public assent to corporate enterprise and the
reluctance to shackle the corporation with initiative-
damaging law have never been greater, even as greater
demands are placed upon it and higher standards articulated for its guidance.

It is of no special importance that business manage-

---

[13]*Ibid,* p. 52.

ment should be classified as a profession. What is important is the aspiration to greater professionalization. As management called "professional" has been separated from ownership and from profit, it has moved toward a more sophisticated practice, toward leadership of change which has transformed our society from a conservative to an innovative orientation, toward more productive relationships with government, toward international activity contributing to the economic development of the world, and toward the action on public problems which we have seen here.

The principal questions which arise when we ask how far we have to go occur in the areas of self-control and social responsibility. It is here that we can expect to find greater progress in the near future. Attention to the quality of organization purpose, to the terms in which it should be judged, may well be the most important next step in the formal progress of business. The influence of professionalization as a social process will be as important a force as have been the "constitutionalizing" of the corporation and the development of due process to regulate its internal life.

We have now before us the major determinants of strategy and the major argument that explicit, sequential attention to four categories of purpose will disentangle an otherwise hopeless confusion. We have not taken up seriously the problems of implementing a suitable strategy. We must turn to these next.

So far, we have considered the principal aspects of formulation, namely, (1) appraisal of present and foreseeable opportunity and risk in the company's environment, (2) assessment of the firm's unique combination of present and potential corporate resources or competences, (3) determination of the noneconomic personal and organizational preferences to be satisfied, (4) identification and acceptance of the social responsibilities of the firm. The strategic decision is one that can be reached only after all these factors have been considered and the action implications of each have been assessed.

The formulation process has an essential creative aspect. In the effort to differentiate our thinking about an individual firm from the conventional thinking of its industry, we must look for new opportunities and for new applications of corporate competence. We must learn how to define a product in terms of its present and potential functions rather than of its physical properties. We must learn a good deal about how to assess the special competence of a firm from its past accomplishments, and how to identify management's values and aspirations. We must be able to rank preferences in order of their strength—our own, among others.

The problem implicit in striking a balance between the company's apparent opportunity and its evident competence between our own personal values and concepts of responsibility and those of the rest of the management, is not an easy one. It is not solved either by familiarity with the basic concepts expounded in this book or by the practice which experience has so far provided. The concepts we have been discussing will help us to prepare to make a decision, but they will not determine our decision for us. Whenever choice is compounded of rational analysis which can have more than one outcome, of aspiration and desire which can run the whole range of human ambition, and of a sense of responsibility which changes the appeal of alternatives, it cannot be reduced to quantitative approaches or to the exactness which management science can apply to narrower questions. A man contemplating strategic decision must be willing to make it without the guidance of decision rules. He must have confidence in his own judgment, which will have been deepened and seasoned by repeated analysis of similar questions. He must be aware that more than one decision is possible and that he is not seeking the single right answer. He can take encouragement from the fact that the manner in which an organization implements the chosen program can help to validate the original decision. For example, the wisdom of deciding to expand from national to international operations may depend on the quality of the implementing action taken.

Some of the most difficult choices confronting a company are those which must be made among several alternatives that appear equally attractive and also equally desirable. Once the analysis of opportunity has produced an inconveniently large number of possibilities, any firm has difficulty in deciding what it wants to do and how the new activities will be related to the old.

In situations where opportunity is approximately equal and economic promise is offered by a wide range of activities, the problem of making a choice can be resolved if reference is made to the essential character of the company and to the kind of company the executives wish to run. The study of alternatives from this point of view will sooner or later reveal the greater attractiveness of some choices over others. Economic analysis and calculations of return on investment, though of course essential, may not crucially determine the outcome. Rather, the log-jam of decision can only be broken by a frank exploration of executive aspirations regarding future development, including perhaps the president's own wishes with respect to the kind of institution he prefers to head, carried on as part of a free and untrammeled investigation of what human needs in what parts of the world the organization would find satisfaction in serving. The fiction that return on investment alone will point the way ignores the values implicit in the calculations and the contribution which an enthusiastic commitment to new projects can make. The rational examination of alternatives and the determination of purpose are among the most important and most neglected of all human activities. The final decision, which should be made as deliberately as possible after a deliberate consideration of the issues we have attempted to separate, is an act of will, desire, and character, as much as of intellect.

The Accomplishment of Purpose: Organizational Structure and Relationships

WE MUST NOW TURN our attention to the concepts and skills essential to the implementation of strategy. The life of action requires more than analytical intelligence. It is not enough to have an idea and be able to evaluate its worth. Men with responsibility for the achievement of goals, the accomplishment of results, and the solution of problems, finally know the worth of a strategy when its utility is demonstrated. Furthermore, a unique corporate strategy determined in relation to a concrete situation is never complete, even as a formulation, until it is embodied in the organizational activities which reveal its soundness and begin to affect its nature.

Interdependence of Formulation and Implementation

It is convenient from the point of view of orderly study to divide a consideration of corporate strategy, as we have divided it, into aspects of formulation and implementation and to note, for example, the requirement of the former for analytical and conceptual ability and of the latter for administrative skill. But in real life the processes of formulation and implementation are intertwined. Feedback from operations gives notice of changing environmental factors to which strategy should be adjusted. The formulation of strategy is not finished when implementation begins. A business organization is always changing in response to its own makeup and past development. Similarly, it should be changing in response to changes in the larger systems in which it moves, and in response to its success or failure in affecting its environment. For the sake of orderly presentation we now focus not on what the strategy should be but on ways to make it effective in action and to alter it as required.

We have already seen that the determination of strategy has four subactivities: the examination of the environment for opportunity and risk, the systematic assessment of corporate strengths and weaknesses, the identification and weighting of personal values, and the clarification of public responsibilities. Implementation may also be thought of as having important subactivities. In very broad terms, these are the design of organizational structure and relationships, the effective administration of organizational processes affecting behavior, and the development of effective personal leadership.

In deciding on strategy, the general manager must force his mind to range over the whole vast territory of the technological, social, economic, and political systems which provide opportunity for his company or threaten its continued existence. When he turns his attention to carrying out the strategy tentatively determined, he addresses himself, within the limitations of his knowledge, to all the techniques and skills of administration. To deal with so wide a range of activity, he needs a simple and flexible approach to the aspects of organized activity which he must take into account. By considering the relationships between strategy and organizational structure, strategy and organizational processes, and strategy and personal leadership styles, the executive should be able to span a territory crowded with ideas without losing sight of the purpose which he seeks in crossing it.

Each of the implementing subactivities constitutes in itself a special world in which many people are doing research, developing knowledge, and asserting the importance of their work over that of other specialists. Thus, the nature of organization, about which every general manager must make some assumptions, is the subject of a richly entangled array of ideas upon which one could spend a lifetime. The design of information systems— particularly at a time when the speed and capacity of the computer fascinates the processors of information—appears to require long study, an esoteric language, and even rearrangement of organizational activities for the sake of information processing. Similarly, performance appraisal, motivation and incentive systems, control systems, and systems of executive recruitment and development all have their armies of theoretical and empirical proponents, each one fully equipped with manuals, code books, rules, and techniques. Leadership itself has been approached less formally, but its nature has been estimated from every point of view ever applied to the interpretation of organized human affairs.

It will, of course, be impossible for us to consider in detail the knowledge and theory which have been developed during the course of a half century of researches in administration. It will be assumed that the reader's own experience has introduced him to the major schools of thought contending in the developing administrative disciplines. Just as the general manager must be able to draw upon the skills of special staffs in leading his company, so he must be able to draw upon these special studies in effecting his own combination of organizational design and organizational practices. The simple prescription we wish to add here is that *the nature of the corporate strategy must be made to dominate the design of organizational structure and processes.* That is, the principal criterion for all decisions on organizational structure and behavior should be their relevance to the achievement of the organizational purpose, not their conformity to the dictates of special disciplines.

Thus, the theses we suggest for your consideration are first that conscious strategy can be consciously implemented through skills primarily administrative in nature and, second, the chief determinant of organizational structure and the processes by which tasks are assigned and performance motivated, rewarded, and controlled should be *the strategy of the firm,* not the history of the company, its position in its industry, the specialized background of its executives, the principles of organization as developed in textbooks, the recommendations of consultants, or the conviction that one form of organization is intrinsically better than another.

The successful implementation of strategy requires that the general manager shape to the peculiar needs of his strategy the formal structure of his organization, its informal relationships, and the processes of motivation and control which provide incentives and measure results. He must bring about the commitment to organizational aims, and policies of properly qualified individuals and groups to whom portions of the total task have been assigned. He must insure not only that goals are clear and purposes are understood, but also that individuals are developing in terms of capacity and achievement and are reaping proper rewards in terms of compensation and personal satisfactions. Above all, he must do what he can to insure that departmental interests, interdepartmental rivalries, and the machinery of measurement and evaluation do not deflect energy from organizational purpose into harmful or irrelevant activity.

To clarify our approach to the problem of adapting the concepts and findings of special disciplines to the requirements of policy, we list here a dozen aspects of implementation which may serve as a convenient map of the territory to be traversed. This list is designed only to make it possible for anyone to use his own specialized knowledge and adapt it, within limits imposed by his own characteristic attitudes toward risk and responsibility, to strategic requirements.

1. Once strategy is tentatively or finally set, the key tasks to be performed and kinds of decisions required must be identified.

2. Once the size of operations exceeds the capacity of one man, responsibility for accomplishing key tasks and making decisions must be assigned to individuals or groups. The division of labor must permit efficient performance of subtasks and must be accompanied by some hierarchical allocation of authority to insure achievement.

3. Formal provisions for the coordination of activities thus separated must be made in various ways, e.g., through a hierarchy of supervision, project and committee organizations, task forces, and other *ad hoc* units. The

prescribed activities of these formally constituted bodies are not intended to preclude spontaneous voluntary coordination.

4. Information systems adequate for coordinating divided functions (i.e., for letting those performing part of the task know what they must know of the rest, and for letting those in supervisory positions know what is happening so that next steps may be taken) must be designed and installed.

5. The tasks to be performed should be arranged in a time sequence comprising a program of action or a schedule of targets. So that long-range planning may not be neglected, this activity should probably be entrusted to a special staff unit. Its influence may be enhanced by attaching it to the president's office, its usefulness by having it work in close cooperation with the line. While long-range plans may be couched in relatively general terms, shorter range plans will often take the form of relatively detailed budgets. These can meet the need for the establishment of standards against which future performance can be judged.

6. Actual performance, as quantitatively reported in information systems and qualitatively estimated through observation by supervisors and the judgment of customers, should be compared to budgeted performance and to standards in order to test achievement, budgeting processes, and the adequacy of the standards themselves.

7. Individuals and groups of individuals must be recruited and assigned to essential tasks in accordance with the specialized or supervisory skills which they possess or can develop. At the same time, the assignment of tasks may well be adjusted to the nature of available skills.

8. Individual performance, evaluated both quantitatively and qualitatively, should be subjected to influences

(constituting a pattern of incentives) which will help to make it effective in accomplishing organizational goals.

9. Since individual motives are complex and multiple, incentives for achievement should range from those that are universally appealing—such as adequate compensation and an organizational climate favorable to the simultaneous satisfaction of individual and organizational purposes—to specialized forms of recognition, financial or nonfinancial, designed to fit individual needs and unusual accomplishments.

10. In addition to financial and nonfinancial incentives and rewards to motivate individuals to voluntary achievement, a system of constraints, controls, and penalties must be devised to contain nonfunctional activity and to enforce standards. Controls, like incentives, are both formal and informal. Effective control requires both quantitative and nonquantitative information which must always be used together.

11. Provision for the continuing development of requisite technical and managerial skills is a high-priority requirement. The development of individuals must take place chiefly within the milieu of their assigned responsibilities. This on-the-job development should be supplemented by intermittent formal instruction and study.

12. Dynamic personal leadership is necessary for continued growth and improved achievement in any organization. Leadership may be expressed in many styles, but it must be expressed in some perceptible style. This style must be natural and also consistent with the requirements imposed upon the organization by its strategy and membership.

The general manager is principally concerned with determining and monitoring the adequacy of strategy, with adapting the firm to changes in its environment, and with securing and developing the people needed to carry out the strategy or to help with its constructive revision. The manager must also insure that the processes which encourage and constrain individual performance and personal development are consistent with human and strategic needs. In large part, therefore, his leadership consists of achieving commitment to strategy via clarification and dramatization of its requirements and value.

We shall return to each of these considerations, looking first at some general relationships between strategy and organizational structure. We shall look also at the need for specialization of tasks, the coordination of divided responsibility, and design of effective information systems.

Strategy and Organizational Structure

It is at once apparent that the accomplishment of strategic purpose requires organization. If a consciously formulated strategy is to be effective, organizational development should be planned rather than left to evolve by itself. So long as a company is small enough for a single individual to direct both planning for the future and current operations, questions of organizational structure remain unimportant. Thus, the one-man organization encounters no real organizational problem until the proprietor's quick walks through the plant, his wife's bookkeeping, and his sales agent's marketing activities are no longer adequate to growing volume. When the magnitude of operations increases, then departmentalization—usually into such clusters of activities as manufacturing, production, and finance—begins to appear. Most functional organizations ultimately encounter size problems again. With geographical dispersion, product complexity, and increased volume of sales, coordination must be accomplished somewhere besides at the top. We then find multiunit organizations with coordinating responsibility delegated to divisions, subsidiaries, profit centers, and the like. The difficulty of designing an organizational structure is basically consequent upon and proportionate to the *diversity* and *size* of the undertaking.

The subject of organization is the most extensive and complex of all the subtopics of implementation. It has at various times attracted the interest of economists, sociologists, psychologists, political scientists, philosophers, and, in a curiously restricted way, of creative writers as well. These have contributed to the field a variety of theoretical formulations and empirical investigations. The policy maker will probably find himself unable to subscribe wholeheartedly to the precepts of any one school of thought or to the particulars of any one model of the firm. Indeed, established theories of the firm are inadequate for general management purposes. The impact of most organizational studies, from the point of view of the eclectic practitioner looking for counsel rather than confusion, has been to undermine confidence in other studies. The activities of present-day social science have in particular badly damaged the precepts of classical scientific management. Progress in the reconciliation of divergent insights into the nature of organization, however, can be expected in due course.

Regardless of disputes about theory among scholars, the executive in, say, a company that has reached some complexity, knows three things. The tasks essential to accomplishing his purposes must in some way be subdivided; they must be assigned, if possible, to individuals whose skills are appropriately specialized; and tasks that have been subdivided must ultimately be reintegrated into a unified whole. The manager knows also that once he lets performance out of his own hands, and once no one in the organization is performing the total task, information about what the left hand is doing must be made available to the right. Otherwise problems and risks cannot be detected and dealt with.

Subdivision of Task Responsibility

In every industry conventional ways of dividing task by function have developed to the extent that the training of individuals skilled in these functions perpetuates organizational arrangements. But identification of the tasks *should* be made in terms of a company's distinctive purposes and unique strategy, not by following industry convention. True, the fact that every manufacturing firm procures and processes raw materials and sells and delivers finished products means that at least production and sales and probably procurement and distribution will always be critical functional areas which must be assigned to specialized organizational units. But these basic uniformities which cut across company and industry lines provide the individual firm with little useful guidance on the issues it finds so perplexing, namely, how much weight to assign to which function, or how to adapt nearly universal structural arrangements to its own particular needs.

A manufacturer who plans to perform services for the government under cost-plus-fixed-fee contracts, to cite a very limited example, feels less need for a fully developed cost control system and cost-related incentives than one whose contracts are governed by a fixed price. To illustrate more broadly the way in which strategic choice determines the relative importance of tasks, consider the manufacturer of a line of industrial products who decides to diversify in view of declining opportunity in his original field. Product improvement and the engineering organization responsible for it become less vital than the search for new products, either internally or through acquisition. But if the latter task is not recognized as crucial, then it is unlikely to be assigned to any individual or unit, but will rather be considered as an additional duty for many. Under the latter circumstances, accomplishment may well be impaired.

Once the key tasks have been identified (or the identification customary in the industry has been ratified as proper for the individual firm), then responsibility for accomplishing these tasks must be assigned to individuals and groups. In addition to a rational principle for separating tasks from one another, the need will soon become apparent for some scale of relative importance among activities to be established.

Distribution of formal authority among those to whom tasks have been assigned is essential for the effective control of operations, the development of individual skills, the distribution of rewards, and for other organizational processes to which we shall soon give attention. The extent to which individuals, once assigned a task, need to be supervised and controlled is the subject of voluminous argument which, temporarily at least, must leave the general practitioner aware that too much control and too little are equally ineffective and that, as usual, he is the man who must strike the balance.

The division of labor is thus accompanied by the specialization of task and the distribution of authority, with the relative importance of tasks as defined by strategy marked by status. The rational principle by which tasks are specialized and authority delegated may be separation by functions, by products or product lines, by geographical or regional subdivision, by customer and market, or by type of production equipment or processes. The intermixture of these principles in multiunit organizations has resulted in many hybrid types of formal structure which we need not investigate. The principal requirement is that the basis for division should be relatively consistent, easily understood, and conducive to the grouping of like activities. Above all, the formal pattern should have visible relationship to corporate purpose, should fix responsibility in such a way as not to preclude teamwork, and should provide for the solution of problems as close to the point of action as possible. Structure should not be any more restrictive than necessary of the satisfaction of individual needs or of the inevitable emergence of informal organization. The design should also allow for more complex structure as the organization grows in size.

As one considers the need to create, build, and develop an organizational structure for his own firm, he will wish to avoid choosing a *typical* pattern of organization on the grounds that it is "typical" or "generally sound." Any preference for divisional versus functional organizations, for decentralized rather than centralized questions, for a "flat" rather than a "steep" or many-stepped hierarchy, should be set aside until the activities made essential by the strategy, the skills available for their performance, and the needs and values of the individuals involved have been identified. The plan one devises should ignore neither the history of the company nor that of its industry, for in ongoing organizations formal structure may not be abruptly changed without great cost. Any new plan devised for gradual implementation should be as economical as is consistent with the requirements for technical skill, proper support for principal functions, and reserve capacity for further growth. The degree of centralization and decentralization prescribed should not turn on one's personal preference, and presumably will vary from one activity to another. Strategic requirements as well as the abilities and experience of company executives should determine the extent to which responsibility for decisions should tend toward the center or toward the field. In a consumer credit company, for example, freedom to extend credit to doubtful risks can really be allowed only to relatively experienced branch managers though company strategy may prescribe it for all.

That so little need be said about the nature of the formal organization, and so much must be determined by the particulars of each individual situation, should not be taken as evidence that formal organization does not matter—a conclusion implied by some students of organizational behavior. On the contrary, progress in a growing organization is impossible without substrategies for organizational development. Restructuring the organization becomes a goal in itself to be worked toward over a period of years—perhaps without the interim publication of the ultimate design.

But though it is impractical, except in cases of harsh emergency, to make sweeping organizational changes with little preparation and upon short notice, this is not to say that no major role is played by structure, by clear and logical subdivisions of task, or by an openly acknowledged hierarchy of authority, status, and prestige—all serving as the conscious embodiment of strategy and the harbinger of growth to come. As we check the relation between strategy and structure, we must ask ourselves always the policy questions: Is the strategy sound and clear? If goals are clear, have the tasks required been clearly identified and assessed for their relative importance? If key activities are known, have they been assigned to people with the requisite training, experience, and staff support they will need? The answers to these questions do not carry one very far along the road toward successful strategy implementation, but they provide a convenient starting point from which the rest of the trip can be made.

Coordination of Divided Responsibility

As soon as a task is divided, some formal provision must be made for coordination. In baseball, the park outside the diamond is subdivided into left, center, and right fields, and a man is assigned to each. But if there is no procedure for handling a ball hit halfway between any two areas, the formal division of labor will help only the hitting team. Most important work of organizations requires cooperation among the departmental specialists to whom a portion of the total task has been allocated. Many forces are at work to make coordination so essential that it cannot be left to chance. For example, the flow of work from one station to another and from one administrative jurisdiction to another creates problems of scheduling and timing, of accommodating departmental needs, and of overall supervision lest departmental needs become more influential than organizational goals.

As soon as a second individual joins the first one in an organization, he brings with him his own goals, and these must be served, at least to a minimal degree, by the activity required of him in service to the organization. As soon as a group of such individuals, different in personal needs but similar in technical competence and point of view is established to perform a given function, then departmental goals may attract more loyalty than the overall goals of the organization. To keep individual purposes and needs as well as departmental substrategies consistent with corporate strategy is a considerable undertaking. It is a major top-management responsibility in all organizations, regardless of the apparent degree of commitment and willingness to cooperate in the common cause.

The different needs of individuals and the distinctive goals of functional specialties mean that, at best, the organization's total strategy is understood differently and valued for different reasons by different parts of the organization. Some formal or informal means for resolving these differences is important. Where the climate is right, specialists will be aware of the relative validity of organizational and departmental needs and of the bias inevitable in any loyalty to expertise.

Formal organization provides for the coordination of divided responsibility through the hierarchy of supervision, through the establishment and use of committees, and through the project form of organization (which, like temporary task forces, can be superimposed upon a functional or divisional organization). The wider the sphere of any supervisor's jurisdiction, the more time he is likely to need to bring into balance aspects of organized life which would otherwise influence performance toward the wrong goals. The true function of a committee—and were this role more widely understood and effectively played, committees would be less frequently maligned—is to bring to the exploration and solution of interdepartmental problems both the specialist and generalist abilities of its members. The need for formal committees would be largely obviated in an ideal organization, where each member was conscious of the impact of his own proposals, plans, and decisions upon the interests of others. To the extent that an individual manager seeks out advice and approval from those whose interests must be balanced with his, he performs in man-to-man and face-to-face encounters the essential coordination which is sometimes formalized in a committee structure.

Coordination can play a more creative role than merely composing differences. It is the quality of the way in which subdivided functions and interests are resynthesized that often distinguishes one organization from another in terms of results. The reintegration of the parts into the whole, when what is at stake is the execution of corporate strategy, is what creates a whole that is greater than the sum of its parts. Rivalry between competing subunits or individuals—if monitored to keep it *constructive* rivalry—can exhibit creative characteristics. It can be the source of a new solution to a problem, one that transcends earlier proposals that reflected only the rival unit's parochial concerns. The ability to handle the coordinating function in a way that brings about a new synthesis among competing interests, a synthesis in harmony with the special competence of the total organization, is the administrator's most subtle and creative contribution to the successful functioning of an organization.

Effective Design of Information Systems

If corporate strategy is to be effectively implemented, there must be organizational arrangements to provide members with the information they will need to perform their tasks and relate their work to that of others. Information flows inward from the environment to all organizational levels; within the company it should move both down and up. In view of the bulk of information moving upward, it must be reduced to manageable compass as it nears the top. This condensation can be accomplished only by having data synthesized at lower levels, so that part of what moves upward is interpretation rather than fact. To achieve synthesis without introducing distortion or bias or serious omission is a formidable problem to which management must remain alert. Well handled, the information system brings to the attention of those who have authority to act not the vast mass of routine data processed by the total system, but the significant red-flag items that warn of outcomes contrary to expectations. A well-designed information system is thus the key to "management by exception." This in turn is one key to the prevailing problem of the overburdened executive.

In the gathering and transmitting of information, accounting and control departments play a major task. One obstacle to effective performance here is devotion to specialty and procedure for its own sake, as accountants look more to their forms than to larger purposes. The Internal Revenue Service, the Securities and Exchange Commission, the Census Bureau, and the Justice Department, all with requirements which must be met, impose uniformities on the ways in which information is collected and analyzed. But nothing in the conventions of accounting, the regulations of the government, or the rapidly advancing mathematical approaches to problem solving in any way prevents the generation and distribution within an organization of the kind of information management finds most useful.

Now, with the speed of the computer, data can be made available early enough to do some good. We shall have much more to say about the uses of information when we turn to the organizational processes that determine individual behavior. It is important to note that the generation of data is not an end in itself. Its function should be to permit individuals who necessarily perform only one of the many tasks required by the organizational mission to know what they need to know in order to perform their

functions in balance with all others, and to gain that over-
view of total operations which will inform and guide the
decisions they have discretion to make. Designing the
flow of information is just as important as choosing a principle of subdivision in outlining organizational structure.
Information is often the starting point in trying to determine how the organization should be changed. It is a way
to monitor the continuing adequacy of strategy and to
warn when change is necessary.

The Accomplishment of Purpose: Organizational Processes and Behavior

OUR STUDY OF STRATEGY has brought us to the prescription that organizational structure must follow strategy if implementation is to be effective. We have seen that structural design inevitably involves (1) a suitable specialization of task, (2) a parallel provision for coordination, and (3) information systems for meeting the requirement that specialists be well informed and their work coordinated. We have seen that a variety of structures may be suitable to a strategy so long as the performance influenced by structural characteristics is not diverted from strategic ends.

We turn now from structural considerations to other influences upon organizational behavior. A logical struc-

196

ture does not insure effective organized effort any more than a high degree of technical skill in individual members insures achievement of organizational purposes. We suggest the following proposition for the test of experience. *Organizational performance is effective to the extent that (in an atmosphere deliberately created to encourage the development of required skills and to provide the satisfactions of personal progress) individual energy is successfully directed toward organizational goals.* Convergence of energy upon purpose is made effective by individual and group commitment to purpose.

Man-made and natural organizational *systems* and *processes* are available to influence individual development and performance. In any organization the system which relates specific influences upon behavior to each other (so as to constitute an ultimate impact upon behavior) is made up of some six elements: (1) standards, (2) measures, (3) incentives, (4) rewards, (5) penalties, and (6) controls. The distinguishing characteristic of a system, of course, is the interaction of its elements. This interdependence will vary from organization to organization and from situation to situation and cannot always be observed, controlled, or completely analyzed.

The familiar processes which bear on performance are (1) measurement, (2) evaluation, (3) motivation, (4) control, and (5) individual development. The most important aspect of a process is the speed and direction of its forward motion and the nature of its side effects. So far as the uniqueness of each company situation allows, we shall look at combinations of these organizational systems and processes in the following order:

1. The establishment of standards and measurement of performance.

2. The administration of motivation and incentive systems.

3. The operation of systems of restraint and control.

4. The recruitment and development of management.

These processes have been studied in detail by specialists of several kinds. We shall not attempt to extract all the wisdom or expose all the folly which, over the years, has accumulated in the study of human relations and organizational behavior. We are now concerned, as always, with the limited but important ways in which specialized bodies of knowledge can be put to use in the implementation of strategy. The idea of strategy will dominate our approach to the internal organizational systems which animate structure, just as it dominated our discussion of the factors that determine structure itself. It may be desirable to point out that our aim is not to coerce and manipulate unwilling individuals. It is instead to support and direct individuals who are at least assenting to or, more desirably, are committed to organizational goals. Commitment to purpose remains in our scheme of things the overriding necessary condition of effective accomplishment.

ESTABLISHMENT OF STANDARDS AND MEASUREMENT OF PERFORMANCE

If progress toward goals is to be supervised at all, it will have to be observed and measured. If it is to be measured, whether quantitatively or qualitatively, there must be some idea of where an organization is compared to where it ought to be. To state where an organization ought to be is to set a standard. A standard takes shape as a projection of hoped-for or budgeted performance. As time passes, positive and negative variances between budgeted and actual performance are recorded. This comparison makes possible, although it does not necessarily justify, relating incentives and controls to performance as measured against standards. For example, managers in the Hilton Hotels group prepare detailed forecasts of their anticipated revenues, costs, and operating profits, all based on past records and future projections that take growth targets into account. The reward system recognizes not only good results but accuracy of forecasting.

It is virtually impossible to make meaningful generalizations about how proper standards might be set in particular companies. It can be said, however, that in any organization the overall strategy can be translated into more or less detailed future plans (the detail becoming less predictable as the time span grows longer), which permit comparison of actual with predicted performance. Whether standards are being set at exactly the proper level is less significant than the fact that an effort is being made to raise them steadily as organizational power and resources increase. External events may, however, invalidate predictions. It must be recognized that for good reasons as well as bad, standards are not always attainable. Hence the need for skill in variable budgeting.

By far the most important problem of measurement is that increased interest in the measurement of performance against standards brings increased danger that the executive evaluation program may encourage performance which detracts from rather than supports the overall strategy.

The temptation to use measurement primarily for the purpose of judging executive performance is acute. The desire to put management responsibility in the ablest hands leads to comparing managers in terms of results.

Failure to meet a standard leads naturally to the assignment of blame to persons. The general manager's most urgent duty is to see that planned results are indeed accomplished. Such pressure, unfortunately, may lead to exaggerated respect for specific measures and for the short-run results they quantify, and thus to ultimate misevaluation of performance.

The problems of measurement cluster about the fallacy of the single criterion.[1] When any single measure like return on investment, for example, is used to determine the compensation, promotion, or reassignment of a manager, the resultant behavior will often lead to unplanned and undesired outcomes. No single measure can encompass the total contribution of an individual either to immediate and longer term results or to the efforts of others. The sensitivity of individuals to evaluation leads them to produce the performance that will measure up in terms of the criterion rather than in terms of more important purposes. Since managers respond to the measures management actually takes to reward performance, mere verbal exhortations to behave in the manner required by long-range strategy carry no weight, and cannot be relied upon to preclude undesirable actions encouraged by a poorly designed measurement and reward system.

Faith in the efficacy of a standard measure like return on investment can reach extreme proportions, especially among men to whom the idea of strategy is apparently unfamiliar. Thus, a visiting top manager from a major automobile manufacturer told a class that the company

---

[1] See John Dearden's "Limits on Decentralized Profit Responsibility" and "Mirage of Profit Decentralization" in E. P. Learned, F. J. Aguilar, and R. C. K. Valtz, *European Problems in General Management,* pp. 570–97. These articles first appeared in the *Harvard Business Review,* July-August, 1962, pp. 81–89; and November-December, 1962, pp. 140–54.

being discussed could solve its apparently bothersome problem of designing an effective relationship between the home office and the branches by giving the branch managers a great deal of autonomy and then judging their performance solely on the basis of return on the capital employed by each. A student who was not convinced answered this argument as follows:

Although this solution to the branch-home office relations problem had merit, it overlooked the fact that the company was dependent for a great deal of its capital on bankers who evaluated the company on bases other than return on investment. If the proposed solution was accepted, the branch manager might increase his return on investment by allowing his delinquency percentage to rise. Rising delinquency percentages might cause the bankers to withhold new credit from the company. The condition could therefore arise in which the branch manager, though carrying out policies which make his performance appear good under the evaluation system being used, would actually be acting in a manner destructive to the welfare of the company as a whole.[2]

Instances in which performance is measured in terms of just one figure or ratio are so numerous as to suggest that the pursuit of quantification and measurement as such has overshadowed the real goal of management evaluation. If we return to our original hypothesis that profit and return on investment are terms that can be usefully employed to denote the results to be sought by business, but are too general to characterize its distinctive mission or purpose, then we must say that short-term profitability is not by itself an adequate measure of managerial performance. Return on investment, when used alone, is another dangerous criterion, since it can lead businessmen

---

[2]David J. Dunn, "Evaluation of Performance" (unpublished student paper). Reproduced by permission.

to postpone needed product research or the moderniza-
tion of facilities in the interest of keeping down the investment on the basis of which their performance is measured. Certainly we must conclude that evaluation of
performance must not be focused exclusively upon the
criterion of short-run profitability or any other single
standard which may cause managers to act contrary to the
long-range interests of the company as a whole.

Our concern for strategy naturally leads us to suggest
that the management evaluation system which plays so
great a part in influencing management performance must
employ a number of criteria, some of which are subjective
and thus difficult to quantify. It is easy to argue that subjective judgments are unfair. But use of a harmful or irrelevant criterion just because it lends itself to quantification
is a poor exchange for alleged objectivity.

Against multiple criteria, it may be argued that they
restrict the freedom of the profit-center manager to produce the results required through any means he elects.
This may of course be true, but the manager who does not
want his methods to be subject to scrutiny does not want
to be judged. Accountants, sometimes indifferent to the
imperfections of their figures and the artificiality of their
conventions, do not always make clear the true meaning
of an annual profit figure or the extent to which a sharp
rise from one year to the next may reflect the failure to
make investments needed to sustain the future of a
product line.

If multiple criteria are to be used, it is not enough for
top management simply to announce that short-term profitability and return on investment are only two measures
among many—including responsibility to society—by
which executives are going to be judged. Such an announcement did not prevent violation of the antitrust

laws by managers in the electrical equipment industry, who believed it was more important for them to produce the expected profit than to inform their superiors that the basis for conducting business both honestly and profitably had disappeared. To give subordinates freedom to exercise judgment and simultaneously to demand profitability produces an enormous pressure which cannot be effectively controlled by endless talk about tying rewards to factors other than profit.

The tragedy of men, honorable in other ways, working for seniors who were apparently unaware of price-fixing practices, should dramatize one serious predicament of the profit-center form of organization, where, characteristically, management expects to solve the problems of evaluation by decentralizing freedom of decisions to subordinates, so long as profit objectives are met. Decentralization seems sometimes to serve as a cloak for nonsupervision, except for the control implicit in the superficial measure of profitability. It would appear to preclude accurate evaluation, and the use of multiple criteria may indeed make a full measure of decentralization inappropriate.

To delegate authority to profit centers and to base evaluation upon proper performance must not mean that the profit center's strategic decisions are left unsupervised. *Even under decentralization, top management must remain familiar with divisional substrategy, with the fortunes—good and bad—that attend implementation, and with the problems involved in attempting to achieve budgeted performance.* The true function of measurement is to increase perceptions of the problems limiting achievement. If an individual sees where he stands in meeting a schedule, he may be led to inquire why he is not somewhere else. If this kind of question is not asked, the answer is not proffered. An effective system of evaluation must include information which will allow top management to understand the problems faced by subordinates in achieving the results for which they are held responsible. And certainly if evaluation is to be comprehensive enough to avoid the distortions cited thus far, immediate results will not be the only object of evaluation. The effectiveness with which problems are handled along the way will be evaluated, even though this judgment, like most of the important decisions of management, must remain subjective.

To quote Dunn once more:

In effect, then, subordinates will not only be judged on the results, but on the effectiveness with which they overcome problems of known magnitude. This involves subjective judgment that raises the question of fairness. I submit the responsibility of top management is to *be fair,* not to evolve a system that proves its fairness beyond the question of a doubt. It is nice to be nice and to establish evaluation systems by which everyone is relieved of fears of personal prejudice and favoritism. It is much more important, however, that an evaluation system contribute to the long-range welfare of the company. If this need necessitates management's requiring subordinates to accept subjective judgment in good faith, then this is what has to be done. If making these judgments requires management's time, then the time will have to be spent.[3]

The process of formulating and implementing strategy, which is supervised directly by the chief executive in a single-unit company, can be shared widely in a multiunit company. Preoccupation with final results need not be so exclusive as to prevent top management from working

---

[3] *Ibid.*

with divisional management in establishing objectives and policies or in formulating plans to meet objectives. Such joint endeavor helps to insure that divisional performance will not be evaluated without full knowledge of the problems encountered in implementation.

When the diversified company becomes so large that this process is impracticable, then new means must be devised. *Implicit in accurate evaluation is familiarity with performance on a basis other than that of accounting figures.*

The formula of evaluation most consistent with the concept of strategy that is outlined in these notes is what is called "management by objectives." Instead of simply evaluating "traits," like some of the older appraisal systems, this process entails at all levels of management a meeting between subordinate and superior to agree on the achievements which the subordinate will try to accomplish during the forthcoming period. The subordinate's suggested objectives are modified if, after discussion, they appear either impractical or understated. They are checked for the contribution they will make to the larger strategy of which they must be a part. They are designed to include quantitatively nonmeasurable items as well as items budgeted in the formal short-term and long-range plans. The problems of successfully designing such a system are easier to see than to solve. Nonetheless, an acceptance of the imperfections and inexactness of such a system, plus a shared interest in the problems to be overcome in serving strategy, make possible a kind of communication which cannot be replaced by the application of a single criterion. Certainly, it is the quality of his objectives and his attempts to overcome obstacles posed by circumstance and competition that is the most important measure of a manager's performance.

MOTIVATION AND INCENTIVE SYSTEMS

The influences upon behavior in any organization are visible and invisible, planned and unplanned, formal and not formal. The intent to measure affects the performance which is the object of measurement; cause and effect obscure each other. The executive who refuses to leave the implementation of strategy to chance has available diverse means of encouraging behavior which advances strategy and deterring behavior which does not. The positive elements, always organized in patterns which make them influential in given situations, may be designated as motivation and incentive systems. The negative elements, similarly patterned, can be grouped as systems of restraint and control. Organization studies have led their authors variously to prefer positive or negative signals and to conclude that one or the other is preferable. The general manager will do well to conclude that each is indispensable.

Whatever the necessity for and the difficulties of performance evaluation, the effort to encourage and reward takes precedence over the effort to deter and restrain. Thus, properly directed, motivation may have more positive effects than control. Certainly, the general manager-strategist, whose own prior experience is likely to have made him intensely interested in the subject of executive compensation, should welcome whatever guidance he can get from researchers or staff assistants working in the field of job evaluation and compensation. Unfortunately, here also the prevailing thinking is often oriented less toward the goals to be sought than toward the requirements of the systems adopted.

The human relations movement has developed convincing evidence that executives, like workers, are influenced by nonmonetary as well as financial incentives. At the same time, it is no longer argued that financial rewards are even relatively unimportant, and much thought has been given to equitable compensation of executives.

Unfortunately for the analyst of executive performance, it is harder to describe for the executive than for the man at the machine what he does and how he spends his time. The terminology of his job description is full of phrases like "has responsibility for," "maintains relationships with," and "supervises the operation of." The activities of planning, problem solving, and directing or administering are virtually invisible. And the activities of recruiting, training, and developing subordinates are hardly more concretely identifiable.

In any case, it is fallacious to assume that quality of performance is the only basis for the compensation of executives. Many other factors must be taken into account. The job itself has certain characteristics that help to determine the pay schedules. These include complexity of the work, the general education required, and the knowledge or technical training needed. Compensation should also reflect the responsibility of the job-incumbent for people and property, the nature and number of decisions he must make, and the effect of his activities and decisions upon profits.

In addition to reflecting the quality of performance and the nature of the job, an executive's compensation must also have some logical relationship to rewards paid to others in the same organization. That is, the compensation system must reflect in some way a man's position in the hierarchy. On any one ladder there must be suitable steps between levels from top to bottom, if incentive is to be provided and increased scope recognized. At the same time, adjustments must be made to reflect the varying contributions that can be expected from individuals in the hierarchy of the staff versus that of the line.

Furthermore, in a compensation system, factors pertaining to the individual are almost as important as those pertaining to performance, the job, or the structure of the organization. A man's age and length of service, the state of his health, some notion of his future potential, some idea of his material needs, and some insight into his views about all of these should influence either the amount of total pay or the distribution of total pay among base salary, bonuses, stock options, and other incentive measures.

Besides the many factors already listed, still another set of influences—this time coming from the external part of the environment—ordinarily affects the level of executive compensation. Included here are regional differences in the cost of living, the increments allowed for overseas assignment, the market price of given qualifications and experience, the level of local taxation, the desire for tax avoidance or delay, and the effect of high business salaries on other professions.

Just as multiple criteria are appropriate for the evaluation of performance, so many considerations must be taken into account in the compensation of executives. The company which says it pays only for results does not know what it is doing.

In addition to the problem of deciding what factors to reward, there is the equally complex issue of deciding what forms compensation should take. We would emphasize that financial rewards are especially important in business, and no matter how great the enthusiasm of a man for his work, attention to the level of executive salary is an important ingredient in the achievement of strategy. Money, it is said, cannot buy happiness. On the other hand, happiness, valuable as it is, cannot buy food, shelter, access to culture, travel, or college educations for one's children. Even after the desired standard of living is attained, money is still an effective incentive. Businessmen used to the struggle for profit find satisfaction in their own growing net worth. Even though taxes may limit asset growth severely, the income is still important. As Crawford Greenewalt says in his *Uncommon Man,* the salary figure provides satisfaction by indicating the worth of the contribution made, even if most of it is paid out in taxes.[4]

There is no question about the desirability of paying high salaries for work of great value. Yet until recently, it was clearly social policy in the United States, as elsewhere, that executive take-home pay be kept at a modest ceiling. As a consequence, profit sharing, executive bonuses, stock options, stock purchase plans, deferred compensation contracts, split-dollar insurance, pension, group term insurance, savings plans, and other fringe benefits have multiplied enormously, and they have been directed not so much toward providing incentive as toward enabling executives to avoid high taxes on current income. It is as incentives, however, that these various devices should be judged. Regarded as incentives to reward *individual* performance, many of these devices encounter two immediate objections, quite aside from the ethics of their tax-avoidance features. First, how compatible are the assumptions back of such rewards with the aspirations of the businessman to be viewed as a professional person? The student who begins to think of business as a profession will wonder what kind of executive will perform better with a profit-sharing bonus than he would with an equivalent salary. He may ask whether a

[4]C. H. Greenewalt, *The Uncommon Man; the Individual in the Organization* (New York: McGraw-Hill, 1959).

doctor should be paid according to the longevity of his patients and whether a surgeon would try harder if given a bonus when his patient survived an operation. Second, how feasible is it to distinguish any one individual's contribution to the total accomplishment of the company? And even if contribution could be distinguished and correctly measured, what about the implications of the fact that the funds available for added incentive payments are a function of total rather than of individual performance? In view of these considerations, it can at least be argued that incentives for individual performance reflect dubious assumptions.

If, then, incentives are ruled out as an inappropriate or impractical means of rewarding individual effort, should they be cast out altogether? We believe not. There is certainly some merit in giving stock options to the group of executives most responsible for strategy decisions, if the purpose is to assure reward for attention to the middle and longer run future. There is some rationale for giving the same group current or even deferred bonuses, the amount of which is tied to annual profit, if the purpose is to motivate better cost control—something surprisingly difficult to do in a business environment marked by booming sales and high income taxes. Certainly, too, incentive payments to the key executive group must be condoned where needed to attract and hold the scarce managerial talent without which any strategy will suffer.

In any case, as we examine the effort made by companies to provide adequate rewards, to stimulate effective executive performance, and to inspire commitment to organizational purposes, we will wish to look closely at the relation between the incentive offered and the kind of performance needed. This observation holds as true, of course, for nonmonetary as it does for financial rewards.

The area of nonmonetary incentive systems is even more difficult to traverse quickly than that of financial objectives. Executives are as much members of the human race as other employees; they are thus as much affected as anyone else by pride in accomplishment, the climate for free expression, pleasure in able and honest associates, and satisfaction in work worth doing.

They are said to be moved also by status symbols like office carpets, thermos sets, or office location and size. The trappings of rank and small symbols of authority are too widely cultivated to be regarded as unimportant, but little is known of their real influence. If individual contribution to organized effort is abundantly clear, little attention is likely to be given to status symbols. For example, the R.&D. executive with the greatest contributions to the product line may favor the "reverse status symbol" of the lab technician's cotton jacket. This is not to say that symbols have no potentially useful role to play. Office decor, for example, can be used to symbolize strategy, as when a company introduces abstract art into its central office to help dramatize its break with the past.

Very little systematic work has been done to determine what incentives or company climate might be most conducive to executive creativity, executive commitment to forward planning, executive dedication to the training of subordinates, or executive striving for personal development and growth. All these are of utmost value, but their impact is long-run and peculiarly intangible. It is well known, however, that the climate most commonly extolled by men in upper management positions is one where they have freedom to experiment and apply their own ideas without unnecessary constraints. This type of positive incentive is particularly suited for use in combination with the "management-by-objectives" approach to the problem of executive evaluation. Given clear objectives and a broad consensus, then latitude can be safely granted to executives to choose their own course—so long as they do not conceal the problems they encounter. In other words, the executive can be presumed to respond to the conditions likely to encourage the goal-oriented behavior expected of him.

We may not always know the influence exerted by evaluation, compensation, and advancement, but if we keep purpose clear and incentive systems simple, we may keep unintended distractions to a minimum. Above all, we should be able to see the relevance to desired outcomes of the rewards offered. The harder it is to relate achievement to motives, the more cautious we should be in proposing an incentives program.

SYSTEMS OF RESTRAINT AND CONTROL

Like the system of incentives, the system of restraints and controls should be designed with the requirements of strategy in mind, rather than the niceties of complex techniques and procedures. It is the function of penalties and controls to enforce rather than to encourage—to inhibit strategically undesirable behavior rather than to create new patterns. Motivation, as we have said, is a complex of both positive and negative influences. Working in conjunction, these induce desired performance and inhibit undesirable behavior.

The need for controls—even at the executive level—is rooted in the central facts of organization itself. The inevitable consequence of divided activity is the emergence of substrategies, which are at least slightly deflected from the true course by the needs of individuals and the concepts and procedures of specialized groups, each with its own quasi-professional precepts and ideals. We must have controls, therefore, even in healthy and competent organizations manned by men of goodwill who are aware of organization purpose.

Like other aspects of organizational structure and processes, controls may be both formal and informal, that is, both prescribed and emergent. Both types are needed, and both are important. It is, however, in the nature of things that management is more likely to give explicit attention to the formal controls that it has itself prescribed than to the informal controls emergent within particular groups or subgroups.

Formal and informal controls differ in nature as well as in their genesis. The former have to do with data that are quantifiable, the latter with subjective values and behavior. Formal control derives from accounting; it reflects the conventions and assumptions of that discipline and implies the superior importance of what can be quantified over what cannot. Its influence arises from the responsiveness of individuals—if subject to supervision and appraisal—to information that reveals variances between what is recorded as being expected of them and what is recorded as being achieved. If the information depicts variances from strategically desirable behavior, then it tends to direct attention toward strategic goals and to support goal-oriented policy. But if, as is more often the case, the information simply focuses on those short-run results which the state of the art can measure, then it directs effort toward performance which, if not undesirable, is at least biased toward short-run objectives.

To emphasize the probable shortcomings of formal or quantifiable controls is not to assert that they have no value. Numbers do influence behavior—especially when pressures are applied to subordinates by superiors contemplating the same numbers. Numbers are essential in complex organizations, since personal acquaintance with what is being accomplished and personal surveillance over it by an owner-manager is no longer possible. As we have seen, the performance of individuals and subunits cannot be left to chance, even when acceptance and understanding of policy have been indicated and adequate competence and judgment are assured. Whether for surveillance from above or for self-contol and self-guidance, numbers have a very meaningful role. We in no way mean to diminish the importance of figures, but only to emphasize that figures must be supplemented by informal or social controls.

Just as the idea of formal control is derived from accounting, the idea of informal control is derived from the inquiries of the behavioral sciences into the nature of organizational behavior. In all functioning groups, norms develop to which individuals are responsive if not obedient. These norms constitute the accepted way of doing things; they define the limits of proper behavior, and the type of action that will meet with approval from the group. In view of the way they operate, the control we have in mind is better described as *social* rather than *informal*. It is embedded in the activities, interactions, and sentiments characterizing group behavior. Sentiments take the form of likes and dislikes among men and evaluative judgments exercised upon each other. Negative sentiments, of great importance to their objects, may be activated by individual departure from a norm; such sentiments can either constitute a punishment in themselves, or can lead to some other form of punishment.

The shortcomings of formal control based on quantitative measurements of performance can be largely obviated by designing and implementing a system in which formal and social controls are integrated. For example, meetings of groups of managers to discuss control reports can facilitate inquiry into the significance of problems lying behind variances, can widen the range of solutions considered, and can bring pressure to bear from peers as well as from superiors. All these features can in turn contribute to finding a new course of action which addresses the problem rather than the figures.

One of the most vexing problems in attempting to establish a functional system of formal and social controls, as we noted in Chapter 5, lies in the area of ethical standards. In difficult competitive situations, the pressure for results can lead individuals into illegal and unethical practices. Instead of countering this tendency, group norms may encourage yielding to these pressures. For example, knowing that others were doing the same thing undoubtedly influenced some electrical industry division managers to flout the antitrust laws when they could not otherwise meet the sales and profit expectations of the home office. On a lesser scale, group norms can be supportive to suppliers making expensive gifts to purchasing agents, or to salesmen offering extravagant entertainment to customers.

Where top management refuses to condone pursuit of company goals by unethical methods, it must resort to penalties like dismissal that are severe enough to dramatize its opposition. If a division sales manager, who is caught having arranged call-girl attentions for an important customer, against both the standards of expected behavior and the policy of the company, is not penalized at all, or only mildly, because of the volume of his sales and the profit he generates, ethical standards will not long be of great importance. If he is fired, then his successor is likely to think twice about the means he employs to achieve the organizational purposes that are assigned to him.

But there are limits to the effectiveness of punishment, in companies as well as in families and in society. If violations are not detected, the fear of punishment tends to weaken. A system of inspection is therefore implicit in formal control. But besides its expense and complexity, such policing of behavior has the drawback of adversely affecting the attitudes of an individual toward his organization. His commitment to creative accomplishment is likely to be shaken, especially if he is the kind of person who is not likely to cut corners in the performance of his duties. To undermine the motivation of the ethically inclined is a high price to pay for detection of the weak.

The student of general management is thus confronted by a dilemma: if an organization is sufficiently decentralized to permit individuals to develop new solutions to problems and new avenues to corporate achievement, then the opportunity for wrongdoing cannot be eliminated. This being so, a system of controls must be supplemented by a selective system of executive recruitment and training. No system of control, no program of rewards and penalties, no procedures of measuring and evaluating performance can take the place of the individual who has a clear idea of right and wrong, a consistent policy for himself, and the strength to stand the gaff when results suffer because he stands firm. This kind of person is different from the human animal who grasps at every preferred reward and flinches at every punishment. His development is greatly assisted by the systems, standards, rewards, incentives, penalties, and controls which permit the application of qualitative criteria and avoid the oversimplification of numerical measures. It is always the way systems are administered which determines their ultimate usefulness and impact.

Recruitment and Development of Management

Organizational behavior, in the view we have just taken of it, is the product of interacting *systems* of measures, motives, standards, incentives, rewards, penalties, and controls. Put another way, behavior is the outcome of *processes* of measurement, evaluation, motivation, and control. These systems and processes affect and shape the development of all individuals, most crucially those in management positions. Management development is therefore an ongoing process in all organizations, whether planned or not. It is appropriate to inquire into the need to plan this development, rather than to let it occur as it will.

In days gone by, before it was generally realized that relying on a consciously designed corporate strategy was far safer and more productive than simply trusting to good luck, a widely shared set of assumptions operated to inhibit the emergence of management development programs. These assumptions have been described as follows:

1. Good management is instinct in action. A number of men are born with the qualities of energy, shrewdness of judgment, ambition, and capacity for responsibility. These men become the leaders of business.
2. A man prepares himself for advancement by performing well in his present job. The man who does best in competition with his fellows is best qualified to lead them.
3. If an organization does not happen to have adequate numbers of men with innate qualities of leadership who

are equal to higher responsibilities, it may bring in such persons from other companies.

4. Men with the proper amount of ambition do not need to be "motivated" to demonstrate the personal qualities which qualify them for advancement.

5. Management cannot be taught formally—in school or anywhere else.[5]

The ideas that we have been examining here suggest that these assumptions are obsolescent. Men are, of course, born with different innate characteristics, but none of these precludes acquiring knowledge, attitudes, and skills which fill the gap between an identifiable personality trait and executive action. Good performance in lesser jobs is expected of men considered for bigger jobs, but different and additional qualifications are required for higher responsibility. Thus, the most scholarly professor, the most dexterous machine operator, and the most persuasive salesman do not necessarily make a good college president, foreman, and sales manager. The abilities that make the difference can be learned from experience or to some extent from formal education. As a substitute for training and supplying the requisite experience internally, companies can import managers trained by competitors, but this approach, though sometimes unavoidable, is risky and expensive. The risk lies in the relative difficulty of appraising the quality of outsiders and estimating their ability to transfer their technical effectiveness to a new organization. The cost lies chiefly in the disruption of natural internal incentive systems.

---

[5]K. R. Andrews, *The Effectiveness of University Management Development Programs* (Boston: Division of Research, the Harvard Graduate School of Business Administration, 1966), p. 232.

The supply of men who, of their own volition, can or will arrange for their own development is smaller than required. Advances in technology, the internationalization of markets, and the progress of research on information processing and organizational behavior all make it absurd to suppose that a man can learn all he will need to know from what he is currently doing. In particular, the activities of the general manager differ so much in kind from those of other management that special preparation for the top job should be considered, unless it is demonstrably impossible.

The multiplication of company-sponsored and university management training programs is evidence that the old idea that managers are born not made has been displaced by the proposition that managers are born with capacities which can be developed. In the process of seeing to it that the company is adequately manned to implement its strategy, we can identify training requirements. In other words, strategy can be our guide to (1) the skills which will be required to perform the critical tasks; (2) the number of persons with specific skill, age, and experience characteristics who will be required in the light of planned growth and predicted attrition; and (3) the number of new individuals of requisite potential who must be recruited to ensure the availability, at the appropriate time, of skills that require years to develop.

No matter what the outcome of these calculations, it can safely be said that every organization must actively recruit new talent if it aims to maintain its position and to grow. These recruits should have adequate ability not only for filling the junior positions to which they are initially called, but also for learning the management skills needed to advance to higher positions. Like planning of

all kinds, recruiting must be done well ahead of the actual
need.

Men with the ultimate capacity to become general managers should be sought out in their twenties, for able men
today in a society in which the level of education as well as
economic means is rising rapidly are looking for careers, not
jobs. In this same spirit companies should recruit—not
to meet the needs for clerk, field salesman, or laboratory
technician alone, but to make an investment in the caliber of
executive who in 25 years will be overseeing an activity not
even contemplated today.[6]

One of the principal impediments to effective execution
of plans is shortage of management manpower of the
breadth required at the time required. This shortage is the
result of faulty planning, not of a natural scarcity of good
raw material. Consider the bank which wishes to open 50
branches overseas as part of its international expansion.
It will not be able to export and replace 50 branch managers unless, years earlier, deliberate attention has been
given to securing and to training banker-administrators.
These are not technicians who know only credit, for example; they must know how to preside over an entire if
small bank, learn and speak a foreign language, establish
and maintain relationships with a foreign government,
and provide banking services not for an exclusively American but for a different group of individual and corporate
customers.

After successful recruitment of candidates with high
potential, speeding the course of management development is usually the only way to keep manpower planning
in phase with the requirements of strategy. Thus, the
recruit should be put to work at a job which uses the

[6]*Ibid.*, p. 240.

abilities he has and challenges him to acquire the knowledge he lacks about the company and industry:

For men educated in this generation sweeping out the stockroom or carrying samples to the quality control laboratory are inappropriate unless these activities demand their level of education or will teach them something besides humility. To introduce the school-trained men of high promise to everyday affairs may mean the devising of jobs which have not existed hitherto. Expansion of analytical sections of accounting and financial departments, projects in market research, rudimentary exploratory investigations in new products departments, process control or data processing projects are all work which will use school-taught techniques and yet require practical and essential exposure to the company and solutions to the problem of establishing working relationships with old hands. Any recruit, no matter how brilliant his academic achievement, has of course much to learn that schools cannot teach him. His seasoning should be accomplished while he works with the power that he has, not doing a sentence of indeterminate length in clerical work of no difficulty.[7]

The manpower requirements imposed by commitment to a strategy of growth mean quite simply that men overqualified for conventional beginning assignments must be sought out and carefully cultivated thereafter. Individuals who respond well to the opportunities devised for them should be assigned to established organization positions and given responsibility as fast as capacity to absorb it is indicated. To promote rapidly is not the point so much as to maintain the initial momentum and to provide work to highly qualified individuals which is both essential and challenging.

[7] *Ibid.*, pp. 240–241.

The rise of professional business education and the development of advanced management programs make formal training available to men not only at the beginning of their careers but also at appropriate intervals thereafter. Short courses for executives are almost always stimulating and often of permanent value. But management development as such is predominantly an organizational process which must be supported, not thwarted, by the incentive and control systems to which we have already alluded. Distribution of rewards and penalties will effectively determine how much attention executives will give to the training of their subordinates. No amount of lip service will take the place of action in establishing effective management development as an important management activity. To evaluate a manager in part on his effort and effectiveness in bringing along his juniors requires subjective measures and a time span longer than one fiscal year. These limitations do not seriously impede judgment, especially when both strategy and the urgency of its implications for manpower development are clearly known.

In designing on-the-job training, a focus on strategy makes possible a substantial economy of effort, in that management development and management evaluation can be carried on together. Thus, a "management-by-objectives" program, already characterized as a most appropriate approach to evaluation of performance, can be simultaneously administered as an instrument of development. For example, in Texas Instruments, Inc., Mr. Pringle could use his conference with his superiors not only to discuss variances from budgeted departmental performance, but also to discover how far his suggested solutions are appropriate or inappropriate and why. In all such cases, discussion of objectives proposed, problems encountered, and results obtained provide opportunities for inquiry, for instruction and counsel, for learning what needs to be done and at what level of effectiveness.

Besides providing an ideal opportunity for learning, concentration on objectives permits delegation to juniors of choice of means and other decision-making responsibilities otherwise hard to come by. Throughout the top levels of the corporation, if senior management is spending adequate time on the surveillance of the environment and on the study of strategic alternatives, then the responsibility for day-to-day operations must necessarily be delegated. Since juniors cannot learn how to bear responsibility without having it, this necessity is of itself conducive to learning. If, within limits, responsibility for the choice of means to obtain objectives is also delegated, opportunity is presented for innovation, experimentation, and creative approaches to problem solving. Where ends rather than means are the object of attention and agreement exists on what ends are and should be, means may be allowed to vary at the discretion of the developing junior manager. The clearer the company's goals, the smaller the emphasis that must be placed on uniformity, and the greater the opportunity for initiative. Freedom to make mistakes and achieve success is more productive in developing executive skills than practice in following detailed how-to-do-it instructions designed by superiors or staff specialists. Commitment to purpose rather than to procedures appears to energize initiative.

A stress on purpose rather than on procedures suggests that organizational climate, though intangible, is more important to individual growth than the mechanisms of personnel administration. The development of each individual in the direction best suited both to his own powers and to organizational needs is most likely to take place in the company where everybody is encouraged to work at the height of his ability and is rewarded for doing so. Such a company must have a clear idea of what it is and what it intends to become. With this idea sufficiently institutionalized so that organization members grow committed to it, the effort required for achievement will be forthcoming without elaborate incentives and coercive controls. Purpose, especially if considered worth accomplishing, is the most powerful incentive to accomplishment. If goals are not set high enough, they must be reset—as high as developing creativity and accelerating momentum suggest.

In short, from the point of view of general management, management development is not a combination of staff activities and formal training designed to provide neophytes with a common body of knowledge, or to produce a generalized good manager. Rather, development is inextricably linked to organizational purpose, which shapes to its own requirements the kind, rate, and amount of development which takes place. It is a process by which men are professionally equipped to be—as far as possible in advance of the need—what the evolving strategy of the firm requires them to be, at the required level of excellence.

Although the processes of recruiting, training, and providing successive job opportunities and challenges are less formal than systems of compensation, control, and performance measurement, they have their own canons and precepts. Their claims to attention and to deference for their own sake must also be subordinated to the requirements of strategy.

The chief executive will have a special interest of his own in the process of management development. For standards of performance, measures for accurate evaluation, incentives, and controls will have a lower priority in his eyes than a committed organization, manned by people who know what they are supposed to do and committed to the overall ends to which their particular activities contribute. The general manager is not blind to the needs of his subordinates to serve their own purposes as well as those of the organization. Wherever conflicting claims are made upon his attention, he requires that they be reconciled in a way which does not obscure organizational objectives or slow down the action being taken to attain them.

The Role of
Leadership in the
Achievement of Purpose

So FAR, we have discussed the formulation and execution of organizational mission without giving much emphasis to the role of the chief executive as a leader in these activities. We have made room, to be sure, for the general manager's personal values, aspirations, and sense of social responsibility, and in this respect we have gone beyond traditional organizational theory. But the personality of the chief executive has to this point been a shadow on our model rather than a part of it.

In simple fact, individual personality leaves a vivid imprint on company affairs. While the mere projection of personal genius or desire, as in the case of Villchur of

226

Acoustic Research, or Jay Monroe of Tensor, does not represent, in our opinion, the most effective relationship of personal leadership to corporate strategy, yet we know that without it there would be no company.

The choice of corporate purpose and the design and administration of organizational processes for accomplishing purpose are by no means impersonal procedures, unaffected by the characteristics of the leader. The study of leadership may be approached from many vantage points. Our concept of strategy can be used once again to give order and perspective to the multiple functions and roles of the general manager and to illumine the range of leadership styles which may either assist or impede organizational performance.

If we look at the roles and activities of a variety of general managers, we can identify three main aspects of leadership. First, we may see the general manager as the architect of strategy. The requirements of this role are analytical ability, creativity, self-awareness, and sensitivity to society's expectations regarding the businessman's broader social responsibilities. Second, we have seen the general manager as an implementer of strategy, that is, as one who supplies organizational leadership. In this area, opportunities for choice are limited. Thus, if strategy is to be maintained, the organizational leader must promote and defend it; he must integrate the conflicting interests which necessarily arise around it; he must see to it that the organization's essential needs are met; and he must be the judge of results. Third, we have seen—but so far have not focused upon—the general manager as *personal leader*.

In the area of personal leadership, our lens narrows to the general manager as a person different from all other persons. Within the range of choice permitted by his own knowledge and command of himself, he achieves a leadership style. This pattern of personal behavior reflects his individuality as much as his office; it does not follow inevitably from the organizational responsibilities he has assumed. The contribution made to company performance, character, and tone by the personal style of the leader and by his concept of his responsibilities will be our final area of inquiry. Thus, we shall proceed in this chapter from the impersonal and general to the highly personal and individual aspects of leadership.

THE GENERAL MANAGER AS ARCHITECT OF STRATEGY

From our assumption that strategy can and should be deliberately determined and specifically articulated, it follows that the general manager must play several roles. These carry with them stringent requirements, even though they imply no specific prescriptions as to what he should do. Thus, to be a leader in the activities of searching out and analyzing strategic alternatives and finally making or ratifying décisions among competing choices, the general manager must be an analyst. His need for intellectual ability equal to this requirement is fundamental; it becomes more compelling as alternatives become more difficult to evaluate and choices become harder to make. The rough-and-ready opportunist is not our preferred prototype, valuable as are his energy and ingenuity.

To find strategic choices that are not routine and to determine a strategy uniquely adapted to external opportunity and internal strengths require the policy-making executive to be an innovator. The entrepreneurial or risk-taking element in strategy formulation often requires the strength to defy the apparent implications of industry trends and to deviate from conventional industry decisions. In folklore psychology, the personalities of the critical analyst and the energetic and creative innovator-entrepreneur are supposed to be antithetical. The strategist, however, must span these opposites. Fortunately, their irreconciliability has been greatly exaggerated.

In addition to powers of analysis and innovation, the strategist must have a sense of personal purpose and an awareness of personal needs. No general prescription can be offered as to what these purposes should be—only the need to bring personal goals into harmony with those suggested by external opportunity and corporate competence. Similarly, awareness of society's expectations requires the analyst-innovator to determine the extent to which he intends to take these expectations into account. In short, in his role as an architect of strategy the general manager examines and becomes informed about the environment external to his company, he examines his own organization, he examines himself, and he determines his own responsiveness to the multiple demands being made upon his company by elements of the community at large. In his role as strategist, he must often think and decide for himself. His role as organization leader is, however, a much less solitary one. As executive in charge of implementation, he is much less the line planner than the doer embroiled on the field with the troops.

The General Manager as Organization Leader

Since strategy does not become either acceptable or effective by virtue of being well designed and clearly announced, the successful implementation of strategy requires that the organization leader act as its promoter and defender. George Romney's efforts in American

Motors to persuade long-time industry executives that the big car was not the key to company success constituted in the 1950–57 era a veritable crusade. Seven years and the departure of a number of top officials were required to effect this change.

The tendency of organizations to veer off course in response to circumstances, special interest, and sudden opportunity means that the general manager must be the defender of strategy. When in a recession year the American consumer turned to the compact car, Mr. Romney probably had little difficulty in promoting his strategy. But when the market changed again, his successor would have the problem of holding the line against those who wanted to follow the market. As Selznick points out in *Leadership and Administration,*[1] a given strategy is subject to being undermined until it has been institutionalized. A neutral body of men does not become a committed organization until goals have been "infused with value." It is the role of the general manager, therefore, not only to make the fundamental analytical-entrepreneurial decisions which are to determine the character of the organization, but also to present these to his organization in a way that appeals to the imagination and engages the support of members whose efforts are essential to success. An organization has to *prove* a strategic decision good or bad, quite apart from its intrinsic merit.

Like any administrator, the chief executive finds himself in the role of mediator and integrator. That is, he must deal with conflict among special interests and among organizational tendencies leading in different directions. For example, in his quest for results, he must become skilled at balancing the need for present profitability

---

[1] P. Selznick, *Leadership and Administration* (Evanston, Ill.: Row, Peterson and Company, 1957).

against the need to invest in future success. With financial analysts seizing on every quarterly report, he must look beyond the pressures they exert to the less insistent demands of long-term development. Similarly, in the administration of organizational systems, he must balance the desirability of uniformity against the requirement for flexibility, the needs of the individual against the needs of the organization, and the interests of special subgroups against the interests of the organization as a whole. The impossibility of resolving such conflicts to the complete satisfaction of all is a fact of life which he must accept. But this inevitability does not permit him to rely upon his own personal identification with one interest or another in place of seeking out the optimum adjustment as dictated by strategic rather than political or expedient considerations. Conflict in organization is inevitable and virtually necessary. Its occurrence, identification, and reconciliation is a daily affair in a healthy, striving association of competent and independent individuals. But progress against competition ultimately requires cooperation of a high order. Commitment to common purpose is ultimately the best assurance that the integration of differences can be achieved.

The general manager cannot effectively lead an organized advance toward chosen goals unless he is aware that his organization has certain needs that are not fulfilled simply by the pursuit of strategy itself. Individuals and departments demand recognition of the validity of their personal and organizational subgoals; individuals further require incentives for performance and a climate conducive to satisfying interpersonal associations and personal development. These things must be given attention for their own sake. Otherwise the intermeshed relationships and processes which are intended to enhance organizational performance will decline into unconstructive conflict and irrelevant activity.

Whether he is conscious of it or not, the general manager is responsible for what is often called the climate of his organization. Intangible as it may be, climate is readily felt. The term "climate" is used to designate the quality of the internal environment which conditions in turn the quality of cooperation, the development of individuals, the extent of members' dedication or commitment to organizational purpose, and the efficiency with which that purpose becomes translated into results. Climate is the atmosphere in which individuals help, judge, reward, constrain, and find out about each other. It influences morale—the attitude of the individual toward his work and his environment.

At the risk of being overprescriptive, but in the hope of suggesting the kind of climate most consistent with successful implementation of strategy, we offer the following description, which is shaped by the requirements of management development:

The most important characteristics of favorable climate from the point of view of management development appear to be these:

1. Absence of political maneuvering for position, with penalties for unfair personal competition and petty conspiracy.
2. Rejection of preferment on grounds other than approval of performance—i.e., blood relationships, friendship, and ethnic, educational, or social background.
3. High standards of excellence explicit in instructions for work as well as in its evaluation; expectations of continuous improvement and competence with increasing experience; disciplined attention to meeting detailed commitments.

4. High value assigned to interpersonal amity and tolerance of individual differences.
5. Willingness to take risks (and acceptance of the inevitability of occasional failure) in delegating responsibility to the relatively inexperienced.
6. Acceptance and encouragement of innovation with consequent freedom to act upon ideas. Disapproval in cases of failure attached to results and causes rather than to departure from conventional practice as such.
7. High standards of moral integrity, including rejection of expediency even at the cost of windfall profits.

The patient establishment and stubborn defense of these values is a practicable undertaking for the leader of an organization. No other duty of his office except perhaps the decision about objectives and strategy is as important.[2]

What is said here about executive development appears to us to apply equally well to a climate generally suitable for the successful accomplishment of strategic purposes. The general manager need not strive to create exactly the climate thus described, but he should determine, rather than leave to chance, the net effect upon people and purposes of the organizational processes over which he presides.

Important as climate is, the general manager must to some extent subordinate sensitivity to climate and members' personal needs to the dominant and inescapable requirements of his role as judge and critic of results. He must *insist upon* the accomplishment which has been projected and must apply the measures, rewards, and penalties available to this end. In this role he is not the supportive figure who listens sympathetically to all the

---

[2]K. R. Andrews, *The Effectiveness of University Management Development Programs* (Boston: Division of Research, Harvard Graduate School of Business Administration, 1966), pp. 247–48.

reasons why something cannot be done. Rather, he holds fast to his conclusion that it will be done—unless prevented by external developments. When a decision is finally taken that reasonable accomplishment can and must take place according to plan, individuals who fail must, if necessary, be replaced. At some point, to preserve commitment and to remain on course, the needs of the organization must be asserted as primary. Commitment to strategy must be tested under adversity before it can be known to be effective. The range of the leadership role—from sensitivity to human needs to insistence upon required performance—has eluded many of the leaders whom we have seen at work. The instinctive, unschooled leader is likely to adopt one role—for example, the role of listener or the role of judge—and to stay in it regardless of circumstances.

The manager must play multiple roles to adapt his leadership to the changing requirements of the situation. He can keep from becoming confused only by steadfastly maintaining his own attention and directing that of others toward the purposes to be achieved. Though he knows that purposes must change and that rigidity is harmful, he does not abandon course at the first sign of trouble. He avoids becoming overpreoccupied by internal conflict. Since executives in departmental positions are much more organizational leaders than architects of strategy, the general manager should expect that solving conflict and satisfying organizational needs should be much less his customary preoccupation than promoting and defending organizational purpose and harvesting results.

THE GENERAL MANAGER AS A PERSONAL LEADER

A wide variety of leadership styles characterizes the behavior of the executive. Under the requirement that he press for planned results, the general manager may behave like a petty tyrant and use his power to abuse those whom he considers offenders. At the other extreme, he may inquire objectively into reasons for failure to achieve results expected, and without raising his voice he may establish a new schedule to match new conditions. He may turn to daily detailed reports to find some discrepancy with which to needle a subordinate, or he may work entirely through intermediaries in calling attention to lapses from standards. It is not appropriate here to review the classifications which have been applied to patterns of leadership. Thus, personalities have been said to range from dominant to inconspicuous; behavior from self-oriented to organization-oriented to people-oriented, or from task-centered to relationship-centered, or from autocratic to democratic to laissez-faire; and approaches from "classical" to "human relations" to "revisionist."[3]

Different kinds of personal leadership may be characterized in various ways, *ad infinitum*. The classification is less important than the possibility that *leadership style is not necessarily innate or entirely dominated by personality*. Even if the roles which the general manager must play are many, and if he must shift from one to another in response to need, yet it may be possible for him to create for himself a distinctive style which will characterize his performance in all his roles—a style which will be both satisfactory to him and functional in its effect upon his followers.

Men in leadership positions are not required to have a personality of any given mold. The effort to relate personality traits to executive effectiveness is no longer pursued

---

[3]See, for example, R. Tannenbaum and W. H. Schmidt, "How to Choose a Leadership Pattern," *Harvard Business Review*, March-April, 1958, p. 95; and W. G. Bennis, "Revisionist Theory of Leadership," *Harvard Business Review*, January-February, 1961, pp. 26 ff.

as naively as once it was. Business leaders generally are likely to be characterized by such qualities as drive, intellectual ability, initiative, creativeness, social ability, and flexibility. These qualities permit a fairly wide range of style so long as it is dynamic and energetic. Obviously, our prescriptions regarding effective leadership would be faulty if they required an individual to do violence to his own personal needs or to convert his natural powers to artifice. Awareness of the impact of his natural forcefulness upon his organization is likely to be adequate for tempering the leader's distinctive behavior to organizational needs.

The general manager will, therefore, examine his own characteristic behavior to try to see whether it meets or complicates the needs of his own organization and whether it directs or distracts the attention given by his followers to organizational goals. To some extent, depending on his powers of self-control, he can modify his behavior in the direction of the need he sees.

The charismatic leader, who, by virtue of his personal magnetism, energy, and force, influences his followers to efforts they would not otherwise make is providing a personal contribution to the implementation of strategy which the less conspicuous administrator cannot effect. Sir Halford Reddish of the Rugby Portland Cement Co., Ltd. is a dramatic personality who, no doubt, has inspired his followers on occasion with admiration, fear, gratitude, and affection. At the same time he has succeeded in dramatizing organizational strategy. He personifies purpose rather than personal power. Although it is not necessary to be flamboyant or eccentric, strategy is well served if the leader is a man whose personal purposes are known and whose commitment to organizational purposes is conspicuous. The sheep in sheep's clothing may be quietly effective, but he does not inspire. When adversity obscures the prospects of success and organizational morale falters, dynamic and articulate leadership—centered upon achievement rather than personality—can make the difference between success and failure.

It must, of course, be admitted that charisma may be more conspicuous than effective. It may evoke in subordinates indignation and amused tolerance rather than heightened accomplishment. The more important danger is that the genuinely strong leader will produce weakness in his organization. Personal strength leads to organizational weakness when fear replaces initiative or awe obscures independent judgment.

Evaluating the contribution that dynamic personal leadership can make to organizational performance, we look for its effects in the dramatization of goals and in the motivation of membership to more than mediocre effort. Strategy is once again the criterion against which we evaluate the effectiveness of the phenomenon under study.

For those who are themselves currently engaged in developing personal values and objectives, it is vitally important to consider the extent to which the role of personal leadership is shaped by personal goals. Harmony between leadership style and the ends sought is essential to effectiveness. It is possible that it can be cultivated.

The Quality of Leadership

We should like therefore to suggest, at the risk of appearing unrealistic, that the principal contribution that personal leadership can make to organizational performance is the projection of the leader's own quality as a person. The depth and durability of his personal values, his personal inner standards of excellence, and the clarity of his integrity can be influential. Corporate purposes are by definition a projection in part of the leader's own personal goals and a reflection of his character. Though the spotlight of fashion today falls upon the business applications of advanced research in the social sciences and in mathematical decision making, we can borrow from Emerson and say that a corporation is essentially the lengthened shadow of a man. It is the mission of the business leader to instill into the organization a tone and quality which, though it may elude measurement, is not unimportant on that account. In the company in which one executive says to another, "Let's have no hanky panky on expense accounts until this stock issue has been completed," it is not hard to project the ethical level of the total enterprise. At the other extreme, the expectations of responsible behavior in the Rugby Portland Cement Company must be as clear as day.

We come to the point where the influence of the leader takes effect through *the person he is* rather than the roles he fills. The character of the leader may be decisive in creating organizational commitment of the depth and quality required by bold purposes or by adverse competitive circumstances. Disagreements about the extent to which ethical behavior can be prescribed do not obscure the plain fact that, for men of goodwill, ethical leadership is more inspiring than that which is not. Few people have problems in distinguishing the difference. The general manager as a personal leader is finally significant not so much because he is the dramatist of organizational progress and performance as because he is the exemplar of the most durable of human aspirations—the desire to devote one's powers to causes worth serving. Purpose attracts commitment when it deserves to do so. Leadership is finally most effective when it clarifies the quality of purpose.

Index

239